THE WHEEL OF FORTUNE

A STUDY OF
ASTROLOGY
GRAPHOLOGY
NUMEROLOGY
DREAMS OMENS
PALMISTRY

1932

KESSINGER PUBLISHING'S
RARE MYSTICAL REPRINTS

THOUSANDS OF SCARCE BOOKS
ON THESE AND OTHER SUBJECTS:

Freemasonry * Akashic * Alchemy * Alternative Health * Ancient Civilizations * Anthroposophy * Astrology * Astronomy * Aura * Bible Study * Cabalah * Cartomancy * Chakras * Clairvoyance * Comparative Religions * Divination * Druids * Eastern Thought * Egyptology * Esoterism * Essenes * Etheric * ESP * Gnosticism * Great White Brotherhood * Hermetics * Kabalah * Karma * Knights Templar * Kundalini * Magic * Meditation * Mediumship * Mesmerism * Metaphysics * Mithraism * Mystery Schools * Mysticism * Mythology * Numerology * Occultism * Palmistry * Pantheism * Parapsychology * Philosophy * Prosperity * Psychokinesis * Psychology * Pyramids * Qabalah * Reincarnation * Rosicrucian * Sacred Geometry * Secret Rituals * Secret Societies * Spiritism * Symbolism * Tarot * Telepathy * Theosophy * Transcendentalism * Upanishads * Vedanta * Wisdom * Yoga * *Plus Much More!*

DOWNLOAD A FREE CATALOG
AND
SEARCH OUR TITLES AT:

www.kessinger.net

CONTENTS

I.	THE HEAVENS	9
II.	THE HOUSES OF THE HEAVENS	15
III.	NATURES OF THE PLANETS AND SIGNS	18
IV.	THE NATURE OF THE ASPECTS	22
V.	MAKING A HOROSCOPE	26
VI.	PLACING THE PLANETS	30
VII.	THE ARABIC POINTS	34
VIII.	JUDGING THE HOROSCOPE	38
IX.	TIMING EVENTS	42
X.	TRANSITS	45
XI.	THE INFLUENCE OF ECLIPSES	49
XII.	SIGNATURE OF THE PLANETS	53
	CONCLUSION	61

PREFACE

THESE pages are written for the general enquirer and not for the advanced student. They are just such as I myself should have wished to have placed before me when, some forty years ago, I began to study what basis of truth there might be in the old-world science of Astrology. It would have saved me much trouble and helped me over the early stages of my research if something as simple and concise had come my way.

This little treatise, therefore, contains nothing that is complex or difficult to follow, and I am disposed to think that this feature will commend itself to the general reader. And yet, perhaps on this account alone, it is capable of carrying the student a great deal further than the more elaborate text-books that are written around controversial points and deal with the more complex problems with which the thorough-paced student is alone concerned.

If the study of these Elements of Astrology should excite a wish for further instruction on the subject, I would recommend my readers to send to my publishers for a complete list of modern works, and this in itself will convey some idea of the wide interest that is now being taken in this most ancient science of the stars.

SEPHARIAL.

CHAPTER I
THE HEAVENS

ASTROLOGY is concerned with the immediate action of the planets of the solar system upon the earth, and hence upon its inhabitants. It is not presumed that we know anything about the *modus operandi* or method of working, but we are concerned solely with the observed effects of the several planets upon the earth. It is probable that the ether of space is the vehicle of the transmission of energy and that its mode of vibration affects our atmosphere. Indeed, we may not strain scientific facts when we affirm that the ether of space is continuous of what we know as inter-molecular ether, which penetrates the densest bodies and the bulk of the earth itself. By this continuity we may reasonably suppose that variations of vibration in spatial ether are communicated to inter-molecular ether, and thus that gross bodies are affected by planetary influence. However that may be, we do not have far to go to prove that the planets have a direct influence upon the earth, and therefore upon all creatures that are earth-born and derive their sustenance from this planet. Newton's hypothesis of interplanetary action has never been scientifically disputed. The solidarity of the solar system is a fact recognised by all the conclusions of modern astronomical science.

But recently it was pointed out by a Fellow of the Royal Astronomical Society that the periodicity of certain terrestrial phenomena could only be accounted for on the hypothesis that the cause of them was outside of the earth's atmosphere. This was a tacit recognition of celestial causation. It passed unchallenged.

The present author has shown that the periodicity of sun-spots coincides to a decimal point with the mean periods of the planets Mars, Earth, Venus and Mercury —the planets that most nearly neighbour the great luminary. This is not a coincidence except in that it coincides with observed facts. Many coincidences make a Law. Astrology is full of such coincidences, and it is only a question as to how many are required to command the consideration of responsible people.

But now let us look at the heavens about which we are expending so much preliminary argument. Turning our faces to the Sun at noon we are facing due South. We find ourselves in the midst of three imaginary circles. The first of these is the meridian, which is the circle passing through the Sun at noon and over our heads. The second is the prime vertical, which extends from due East, over our heads, to the Western horizon. The third is the circle of the horizon, which extends in all directions as far as the eye can reach. These three circles form the basis of the horoscope and may be represented by the figure on opposite page.

All the stars and planets rise in the East at the point A, which is the Ascendant. They culminate or reach their highest point at the M.C. (medium cœli) or Midheaven. They set at the point D, which is the Desendant or West Horizon.

This apparent motion of the celestial bodies about the earth is due to the rotation of the earth on its axis from West to East, by which the stars appear to go from

THE HEAVENS 11

East to West. For half the day they are above the horizon and for the other twelve hours they are below the horizon. This is always the case when they rise due East, but when they rise in the N.E. they will set in the N.W., and when they rise in the S.E. they will set

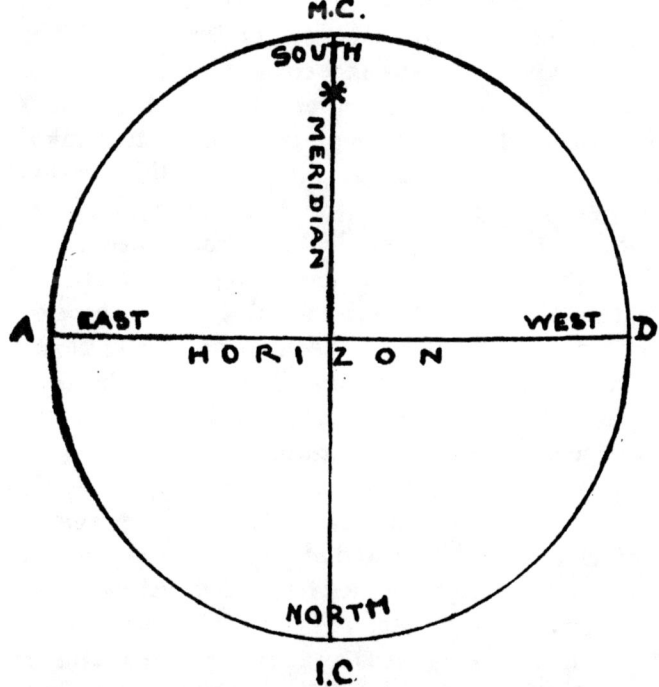

in the S.W., and this difference will make the diurnal or day period longer or shorter, as the case may be, than the nocturnal or night period. Thus, all planets in North declination, that is, moving along a line north of the equator, have a longer period above the earth than below it, and those that have South declination are for a shorter time above the earth than below it. This difference is observed in regard to the Sun, which in the summer time has North declination and stays for a longer time above the horizon than below it, and in the winter time the reverse of this. It is the same with all the planets. The cause of this is the inclination of the earth's axis, which is inclined at an angle of about 23° 27′ to the plane of the ecliptic or Sun's path. The Sun and planets all cross the equator in the course of their revolutions at various angles. The ecliptic, or Sun's path through the zodiac, represents the astronomical equator, and the orbits of the planets cross this celestial equator at different angles, and the distance of the planet from the ecliptic is called celestial latitude.

Thus we have declination answering to geographical latitude, and this is the distance of a planet above or below the earth's equator. When above, it is in North declination, and when below in South declination. We have also celestial latitude, which is a planet's distance above the ecliptic or celestial equator.

You will find these distances marked day by day in any ephemeris of the planet's motion. An ephemeris (Gr. *ephemera*—a day) is a daily position-chart of the celestial bodies. It is compiled from official astronomical publications, and shows the positions of the Sun, Moon, and planets in the heavens as seen from the centre of the earth. These are called "geocentric" positions. A different point of view would change their apparent places, and if you were on the Sun you would observe the heliocentric positions only. In Astrology we are concerned only with the question of how the planets affect the earth, and therefore we take the positions as seen from the earth.

THE HEAVENS

The position of a planet, as marked in the ephemeris for any day at noon, is its place in the zodiac. This is a broad belt extending 27 degrees above and below the equator. The Sun's path extends from 23° 27' below to 23° 27' above, and the point where it crosses the equator is called the equinox, because at this point there is equal day and night on all parts of the earth. The Ecliptic is divided into twelve equal parts, called Signs, counting from the equinox. These signs of the zodiac are known by hieroglyphic symbols, and they are named as follows :—

Name.	Meaning.	Symbol.
Aries	Ram	♈
Taurus	Bull	♉
Gemini	Twins	♊
Cancer	Crab	♋
Leo	Lion	♌
Virgo	Virgin	♍
Libra	Balance	♎
Scorpio	Scorpion	♏
Sagittarius	Archer	♐
Capricornus	Goat	♑
Aquarius	Waterman	♒
Pisces	Fishes	♓

From Aries to Virgo are northern signs, because the Sun is north of the equator when he is in these signs. The others are southern signs for a similar reason. The Equinoxes are the points Aries 0 and Libra 0. They mark the position of the Sun in the ecliptic when it crosses the equator, and are called the Vernal Equinox and Autumnal Equinox respectively. The first point of Cancer is called the Summer Solstice,

14   ASTROLOGY SIMPLIFIED

and the first of Capricorn is called the Winter Solstice. They mark the position of the Sun at its highest point above the equator and its lowest below the equator.

The following diagram will assist in conveying these ideas :—

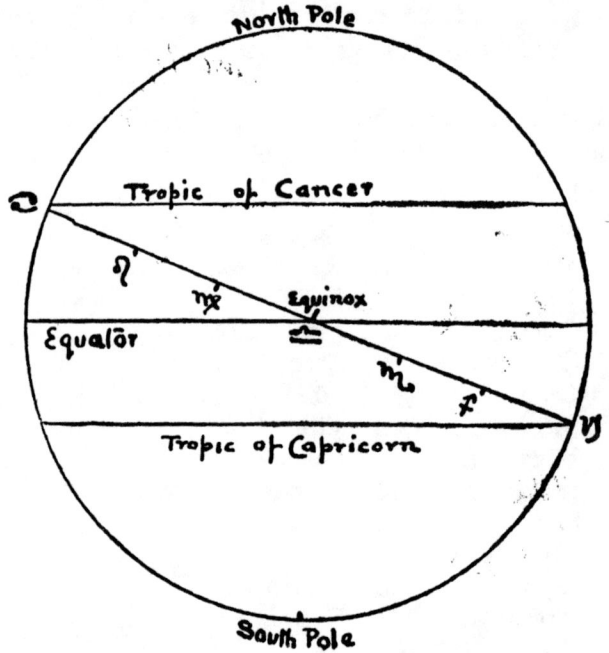

The planets also have their appropriate symbols, which are as follows :—

Neptune, ♆. Uranus, ♅. Saturn, ♄. Jupiter, ♃. Mars, ♂. Venus, ♀. Sun, ☉. Mercury, ☿. Moon, ☽.

The planets known to the ancients were Saturn, Jupiter, Mars, Sun, Venus, Mercury, and the Moon. It has been frequently mentioned by modern astronomers that the inclusion of the planet Mercury, which is so near to the Sun as to be seldom seen, was evidence of the astuteness of the ancients, "whose lynx eyes suffered nothing to escape them."

CHAPTER II

THE HOUSES OF THE HEAVENS

WE now come to the division of the prime vertical or circle of observation, which my readers will recognise as that circle which passes immediately overhead from East to West when facing due South.

This is divided for astrological purposes into twelve equal parts, called "Houses," which answer to the twelve signs of the zodiac. These Houses remain fixed in regard to any locality, while the signs of the zodiac, carrying with them the several planets, pass through them in the course of twenty-four hours.

To each of these Houses the astrologer ascribes a definite rulership or significance, and they may be regarded as the departmental limits of the many affairs to which they are allocated.

The Houses are counted from the East horizon, round through the North to the West horizon, and thence through the South back again to the East horizon, as shown on page 16.

SIGNIFICATIONS.

The First House rules over the Life and Person of the subject born.

The Second House has relation to the financial affairs and monetary possessions, questions of buying and selling, trade returns.

The Third House governs blood relations, various means of communication, such as post, rail, coach, motor, telegraph, telephone, etc., short journeys.

The Fourth House rules the Mother in a male and the Father in a female horoscope, real estate, the

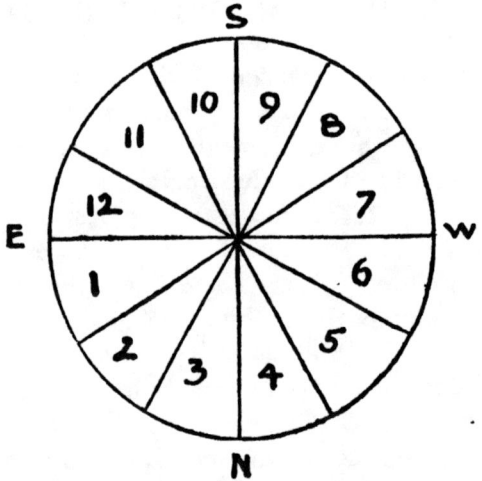

residence, lodging or abode of the person. Its final significance is the grave or end of life.

The Fifth House governs sports and speculation, education and training, invention, youthful associations and love affairs, progeny.

The Sixth House denotes health, servants, furniture, the menage, and such things as food, clothing, etc., which contribute to the personal comfort and well-being. Employees generally. Occupation.

The Seventh House denotes contracts, and more especially marriage and partnerships whatsoever.

The Eighth House denotes losses (as the 2nd denotes gains) and so far as the person is concerned has significance of the nature of death. It also denotes legacies and dowries, and the financial affairs of those entering into partnership.

The Ninth House denotes long journeys, voyages, foreign affairs, philosophy, religion, other-world experience, insurance, legal matters.

The Tenth House shows the position, credit and standing of the subject, honours, attainments.

The Eleventh House indicates friends and associates, confidants, emoluments of office, gain from business, social affairs, supporters and advocates.

The Twelfth House denotes barriers, impediments, closure, confinement, limitations, secret enemies, unseen dangers.

The planets occupying these Houses at birth, and the signs in which they are placed, enable us to forecast the general events of the life. Thus, if Saturn is in the Midheaven at birth, it is a sign of exaltation, followed by disgrace and loss of office and position. If Jupiter is in the 11th House the subject will have many friends and supporters, and his position will be such as to afford handsome emoluments.

In order more clearly to understand how the planets work in the several Houses, it will be necessary to know the simple natures of the planets themselves, and also the nature of the aspects they hold to other planets in the horoscope. This must be our next section.

CHAPTER III

NATURES OF THE PLANETS AND SIGNS

THE ancients knew nothing of the planets Neptune and Uranus. The latter was discovered by observation of certain irregularities in the motion of the planet Saturn, which, according to the ancients, was the outermost of the planets of the solar system. The planet was discovered in 1781, by Sir Frederick William Herschel, who called it Georgium Sidus, in honour of King George III, but afterwards it was called Herschel, after its discoverer, and now is known by its classical name of Uranus, the father of Saturn. Neptune was discovered in 1846 by the perturbations of the planet Uranus, and was named after the Roman god of the Ocean and the Greek god Poseidon. He corresponds to the Hindu god Varuna, who rules over the ocean of space, just as Uranus corresponds with Indra, the god of the heavens.

Neptune denotes instability, uncertainty, chaos, confusion, deceptions, ambushes, schemes and plots. Depletion, fraud and leakage.

Uranus denotes fractures, dislocations, breaking down of existing conditions, sudden catastrophe, alienation, parting and sundering of ties, lesions, litigation, ruptures and separations.

Saturn shows privations, coldness, want, degradation, loss, sorrow, and all kinds of physical, financial and mental stress.

Jupiter denotes increase, profit, expansion, affluence, good fortune, great opportunities, influence, power, success.

Mars denotes hurt by strife or accident, friction, enmity, energy, effort, strain, enterprise, daring, ambition and prowess.

The *Sun* denotes honours, dignities, position, fame, renown, grandeur, pride, favours of high personages.

Venus indicates placidity, peace, fruitfulness, docility, the fine arts, pleasures, social attainments, geniality, affection and love.

Mercury shows activity, business, trade, commerce, the sciences, literature, travelling, languages.

The *Moon* denotes changes, female influence, public affairs, the people, voyaging, versatility, adaptation.

To summarise these attributes and ascriptions of the several planets, we may say that each planet has two aspects or faces, one of which is normal and the other abnormal. It depends on the sign occupied by the planet, and the relation it bears to other planets in the horoscope, as to whether it will express itself along normal or abnormal lines. Thus:—

Normal.	Planet.	Abnormal.
Genius, inspiration	Neptune	Dementia, chaos
Construction	Uranus ...	Destruction
Stability ...	Saturn ...	Privation
Prosperity	Jupiter ...	Extravagance
Energy ...	Mars ...	Strife
Dignity ...	Sun ...	Vanity
Peace ...	Venus ...	Indolence, luxury
Alertness ...	Mercury	Agitation
Adaptation	Moon ...	Vacillation

The planets act more forcibly when in congenial signs, that is to say, in signs of the zodiac whose natures agree more or less with the nature of the planet. Thus :—

Saturn has affinity with the earthy signs Virgo, Capricorn and Taurus.

Jupiter is best placed in one of the watery or fruitful signs, namely, Cancer, Scorpio and Pisces.

The *Moon* has the same affinities as Jupiter.

Mars is exalted in the fiery signs, Aries, Leo and Sagittarius.

The *Sun* has the same affinities as Mars.

Venus attains its highest expression in one of the airy signs, Gemini, Libra and Aquarius.

Mercury has a variable nature, akin on the material side of life to Saturn, and on the intellectual side to Venus.

This planet partakes of the nature of that planet with which it is in closest aspect at birth, or when not in aspect, with the nature of the planet in whose sign it may be found at the time. The planet is called the "Messenger of the Gods," because he speaks all languages. He is also Merx (trade), and thus is identified with the "winged messenger" or the ship of commerce.

The signs ruled by the planets are as follows :—

Aries is ruled by Mars. Taurus by Venus. Gemini by Mercury. Cancer by the Moon. Leo by the Sun. Virgo by Mercury. Libra by Venus. Scorpio by Mars. Sagittarius by Jupiter. Capricorn by Saturn. Aquarius by Saturn. Pisces by Jupiter.

Thus each of the planets has two signs over which to rule and the Moon and Sun one each. But, according to more modern experience, it seems probable that

NATURES OF THE PLANETS AND SIGNS

Uranus has dominion in the sign Aquarius and Neptune in Pisces. So that, counting backwards against the order of the signs, we have the following orderly array of the planets in relation to their respective dominions:—

Pisces	Neptune
Aquarius	Uranus
Capricornus	Saturn
Sagittarius	Jupiter
Scorpio	Mars
Libra	Venus
Virgo	Mercury
Leo	Sun
Cancer	Moon
Gemini	Mercury
Taurus	Venus
Aries	Mars

Uranus is held to be a higher octave of the planet Mercury, and Neptune that of Venus. Certainly it appears that the higher characteristics of Mercury are related to the planet Uranus and those of Venus to Neptune. I think it most reasonable to presume two distinct types of each planet, as, for instance, the sensuous type of Venusian under Taurus, and the etherial type under Libra; the ecclesiastical and judicial type of Jupiter under Sagittarius, and the *bon vivant* under Pisces; and so of the rest.

The signs of the zodiac are divided into two classes: Constitutional and Elemental. The Constitutions are as here given:—

Cardinal or Movable Signs—Aries, Cancer, Libra and Capricorn

Fixed or Foundation Signs—Taurus, Leo, Scorpio, Aquarius.

Common or Flexed Signs—Gemini, Virgo, Sagittarius, Pisces.

The Elemental Natures of the Signs are these :—

Fiery Signs—Aries, Leo, Sagittarius.
Earthy Signs—Taurus, Virgo, Capricornus.
Airy Signs—Gemini, Libra, Aquarius.
Watery Signs—Cancer, Scorpio, Pisces.

Male signs are Aries, Gemini, Leo, etc., each alternate sign from Aries being male, and the rest, namely, Taurus, Cancer, etc., are female.

THE BODY AND THE SIGNS.

Aries rules the head, Taurus the ears, lower jaw and throat, Gemini the arms, Cancer the chest, Leo the back and heart, Virgo the bowels, Libra the groins and kidneys, Scorpio the excretory process, Sagittarius the thighs, Capricornus the knees, Aquarius the shins and ankles, Pisces the feet.

CHAPTER IV

THE NATURE OF ASPECTS

EVERY circle is divided into 360 degrees. For astrological purposes this is divided into several arcs called Aspects. The triangle of equal sides is called an equilateral triangle, and if this be inscribed in a circle, each side will be the chord of an arc of 120 degrees. This is called the *trine* aspect, because it is one-third of the circle.

Half this is the *sextile*, or one-sixth of the circle, equal to 60 degrees.

Half this again is 30 degrees, called the *semisextile*.

All these are benefic or harmonising aspects and import good effects when existing in the horoscope.

The trine is the most powerful, then the sextile, and lastly the semisextile.

A line dividing the circle into two equal parts is called the diameter, or cross-measure. It bisects the circle into arcs of 180 degrees each. This is called the *opposition* aspect. Half this is the quadrate or *square*, being equal to 90 degrees. Half this again is the *semisquare* aspect of 45 degrees. By adding the square and the semisquare together we get another aspect, called the *sesquare*, or sesquiquadrate, of 135 degrees in extent.

All these are evil or malefic aspects, and of these the opposition is the strongest, then the square, and the sesquare and semisquare of 135 degrees and 45 degrees are of inferior power.

Expressed in signs of the zodiac these aspects may be more easily estimated, thus :—

Good Aspects.

Trine of 120 degrees is equal to 4 signs.
Sextile of 60 degrees is equal to 2 signs.
Semisextile of 30 degrees is equal to 1 sign.

Evil Aspects.

Opposition of 180 degrees is equal to 6 signs.
Sesquare of 135 degrees is equal to 4½ signs.
Square of 90 degrees is equal to 3 signs.
Semisquare of 45 degrees is equal to 1½ signs.

As a memory aid it may be well to note that the trine aspect involves two signs of the same element, as Aries and Leo, or Leo and Sagittarius, or Sagittarius and Aries, all of which are *fiery* signs. The airy, watery, and earthy signs are likewise all in trine aspect to those of the same element.

Again, signs of the same Constitution, as Fixed, Flexed or Cardinal, are in square to one another.

Moreover, signs in sextile are sympathetic, being of elemental nature agreeable to one another. Thus, the signs of water and earth are in sextile, as Scorpio and Virgo, Taurus and Pisces, etc. Also fiery signs are in sextile to airy signs. The earth cannot but be sustained by water, as fire is by air.

Now all aspects are the angles or complemental angles of regular polygons inscribed in a circle. They are, moreover, those angles at which the superior metals crystallise. Water crystallises at an angle of 60 degrees. This is the chemistry of Nature, as expressed in the learning of the ancients.

Positions

are often included in "aspects." They are:—

The *Conjunction*, as when two bodies are within orbs of one another, and in the same part of the heavens.

The *Parallel*, as when two bodies hold the same degree of declination, both being either N. or S. of the equator. They then traverse the same parallel, and by

THE NATURE OF ASPECTS

the diurnal rotation of the earth on its axis are carried over the same line from East to West, and they act as if in conjunction.

Mutual Disposition, as when two planets are in one another's signs, as Venus in Cancer, ruled by the Moon, and the Moon in Taurus, ruled by Venus. They then act as if in conjunction.

Orbs.

The orbs of the planets are of the following dimensions, within which radius they are capable of acting as if in conjunction. The Sun, 15 degrees. The Moon, 12 degrees. Jupiter, 10 degrees. Saturn, 9 degrees. Venus, 8 degrees. Mars, 7 degrees. Mercury, Uranus and Neptune, 5 degrees each. At these distances from any point the several planets are in conjunction. Thus, if the Sun were in Aries 1 and Uranus in Aries 16, the Sun would be "within orbs" of Uranus. Uranus, however, has an orb of 5 degrees, and in order to find at what distance they begin to react on one another, we must add their orbs together and divide by two. Thus, Sun 15 degrees plus Uranus 5, gives 20 degrees, and half this is 10, at which distance the two bodies operate as if in conjunction. But if the Sun is 15 degrees from the Midheaven or the Ascendant of the horoscope, there can be no reaction, because these degrees have no dynamic power, but have only a significance and are really neutral points. The Sun and Moon are thus found to react on one another at a distance of twelve and a half degrees, and this coincides with the ecliptic orb of the Moon, at which distance from the Node it may be eclipsed when in opposition to the Sun.

Symbols of Aspects.

Trine aspect is thus indicated	△
Square	□
Sesquare	⚄
Semisquare	∠
Sextile	✶
Semisextile	⚺
Opposition	☍
Parallel	P.
Conjunction	☌
Mutual Disposition	M.D.

CHAPTER V

MAKING A HOROSCOPE

A HOROSCOPE is an astronomical figure set for any given time and place. It does not purport to be more than a general map of the heavens, showing the positions of the planets and signs of the zodiac in relation to a particular place at a set time. It is easily constructed.

Take an ephemeris for the year of birth (which can be obtained from my publishers), it will be seen that opposite to the date of birth the Sidereal Time is given. The whole circle of the Sun's course during the year is divided into 24 hours, so that there are 15 degrees to each hour. Then, if the time of birth is p.m. or after noon, you merely add the time to the Sidereal Time (S.T.) given in the ephemeris for that date, and to this you add also 10 seconds for each hour after noon. The sum of these three factors will be the Right Ascension of the Midheaven at the time of birth.

MAKING A HOROSCOPE

Suppose, however, that the time of birth is a.m. or before noon. Then subtract the hours before noon and also 10 seconds for correction for each hour. Thus, if the time of birth is 6.30 a.m., it will be 5 hours 30 minutes before noon, so we have to take 5 hours 30 minutes from the S.T. and also 55 seconds for correction. We then have the R.A. of the Midheaven at birth, if the birth occurred at Greenwich or near it.

Let us suppose, however, that the birth was at Liverpool, and that the time of the clock was 10.30 a.m., or 1 hour 30 minutes before noon. Suppose the date to be 1st January, 1880. Now, when it is noon at Greenwich (for which meridian the ephemeris is made), it wants 12 minutes to noon at Liverpool. Therefore the first correction is to take away 12 minutes from the stated Greenwich time of birth, and it thus becomes 10.18 local time, or 1 hour 42 minutes before local noon.

	h.	m.	s.
The S.T. for 1st Jan., 1880, is seen to be ...	18	42	7
From this take 1h. 42m., and correction 16s.	1	42	16
Right Ascension of Midheaven at birth	16	59	51

At the end of the ephemeris there are Tables of Houses, and against the Sidereal Time 16h. 59m. 51s. we find the sign Sagittarius 16 degrees. This was on the Midheaven at birth. Against this, under the heading of Ascendant, we find the sign Aquarius 23 degrees 2 minutes, and this was the degree of the zodiac rising at the time of birth.

Now if we make a cross by a perpendicular line representing the meridian, and one horizontal denoting the horizon, we shall have a true astronomical figure of the heavens, so far as our calculation has extended. But in Astrology we have twelve divisions of the heavens and not four. Hence we have to divide each quadrant into three equal parts, called Houses. This can most effectively and easily be done by finding the number of degrees of the zodiac between Sagittarius 16 and Aquarius 23. We know that there are 30 degrees in each sign, and as 16 of Sagittarius have already passed the meridian, there must be 14 more to pass in order to complete that sign. Then there are 30 in the next sign Capricorn, and 23 in Aquarius up to the point of rising, making in all:—

Sagittarius	14
Capricorn	30
Aquarius	23
	67

and this being divided by 3 gives 22 degrees for each House. If we add 22 to Sagittarius 16 we shall have Capricorn 8 on the cusp of the 11th House. A further 22 degrees being added gives us Aquarius 0, and a further 22 brings us to the Ascendant as nearly as possible.

From this point we enter another quadrant, and this has to be dealt with separately. Two quadrants together are equal to 180 degrees, and one-sixth of this is 30, so that if the signs were equally distributed through the Houses each would embrace 30 degrees. As it is we find that there were only 22 on each House in the quadrant between the Midheaven and Ascendant, and therefore there must be 38 in each of the Houses in the adjacent quadrant.

MAKING A HOROSCOPE 29

We therefore add 38 degrees, or one sign and 8 degrees to Aquarius 23, and we get Aries 1 on the cusp of the 2nd House, and adding still further another 38

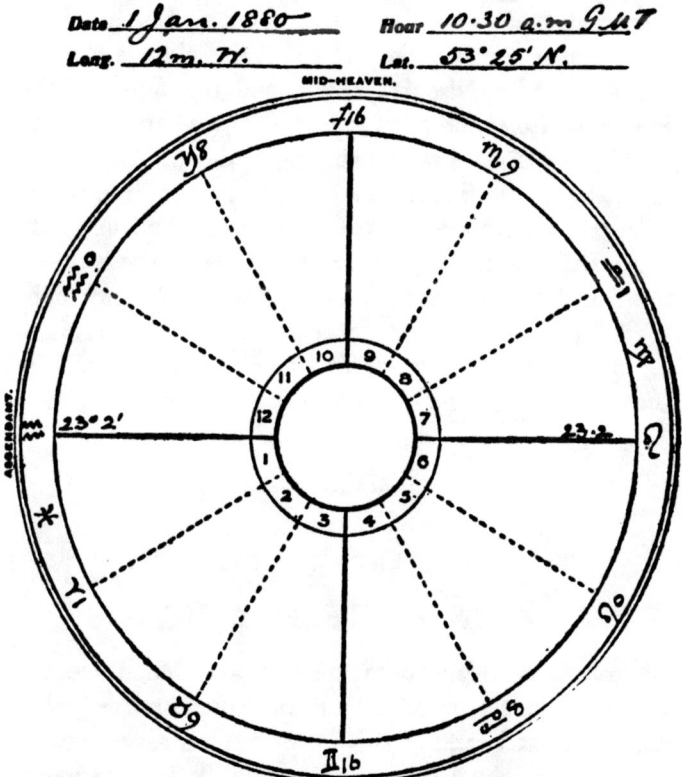

degrees we come to Taurus 9, which is therefore on the cusp of the 3rd House.

The rest of the Houses are occupied by the opposite signs to these, and the same degrees. Thus, Sagittarius 16 being on the Midheaven, Gemini 16 will be on the

Nadir or cusp of the 4th House, and Capricorn 8 being on the cusp of the 11th, Cancer 8 must be on the cusp of the 5th House, and so of the rest.

The figure on the previous page shows the distribution of the Signs through the Houses at 10.30 a.m. Greenwich time, on 1st January, 1880, at Liverpool.

It is now only necessary to place the planets in their proper places in the horoscope and the figure of the heavens will then be complete. This we can do by the aid of an ephemeris which gives the places of the planets in the zodiac for each day at noon throughout the year. These ephemerides are published annually for the next year, and the most complete of these is that known as "Raphael's Ephemeris," issued by my publishers for any year from 1800 up to the present date. In casting a horoscope for one's birth, therefore, it is necessary to have the ephemeris for the year of birth.

CHAPTER VI
PLACING THE PLANETS

FOR astrological purposes the Sun and Moon are regarded as planets, inasmuch as they appear to revolve around the earth, and as this latter is the passive centre of any action which these bodies may be said to exert upon it, the places of the planets are taken as seen from the centre of the earth, and not astronomically, as seen from the centre of the Sun. This is the difference between the geocentric and heliocentric longitudes of

PLACING THE PLANETS

the planets. The difference is known as parallax, and amounts to more or less according to the relative distances of the planets.

Having found the date of birth in the ephemeris, under the symbol of the Sun you will find the longitude of the Sun at noon on that date. This has to be corrected for the time before or after noon at which the birth took place. The Sun's mean motion is at the rate of about 5' in two hours.

Next look to the Moon under the symbol of the Moon, and against the date of birth will be found its longitude. This has also to be corrected. Take the number of hours and minutes before or after noon for which you are making the horoscope, and divide these by two, calling them degrees and minutes of longitude. This must be subtracted from the Moon's place at noon, if the birth was before noon, or added to it if the birth was after noon. This will give a rough estimate of the Moon's place at birth.

The planets, Neptune, Uranus, Saturn, Jupiter, Mars, Venus and Mercury, must all be dealt with similarly, equation of longitude being made in each case for the time of birth.

The precise rule is as follows: Find the difference of longitude from noon on the day of birth to noon of the preceding or following day, according as the birth was a.m. or p.m. Then this will be the diurnal motion of the planet, and proportion can be made for the Greenwich time of birth.

Note that the time must always be Greenwich time and not local time, as the ephemeris is calculated for Greenwich. At the end of the ephemeris will be found a set of Diurnal Logarithms, the use of which will very materially reduce the work of calculation. Thus, if we add the logarithm of the planets motion to the logarithm of the time (before or after noon) we shall have the logarithm of the motion for that time, and this being applied to the longitude of the planet at noon will give the true place for the hour and minute required.

Adhering to our date, 1st January, 1880, at 10.30 a.m. Greenwich time, we may now calculate the places of the planets:—

The *Sun*.—Long. at noon Capricorn 10.31
    Motion per day 61′ for which logarithm is   1.3730
    Time before noon 1h. 30m. .   „   1.2041

    Motion of Sun is 4′   . . „   2.5571

As the time is before noon we subtract it from the Sun's place at noon and get its true longitude in Capricorn 10.27. This is marked in the horoscope.

The *Moon*.—Long. for noon Leo 24. 5
    Previous noon   11.24

    Diurnal motion   12.41 logarithm 2868
    Time as before   .   „   1.2041

    Moon's motion 0° 46′   „   1.4909

This taken from Leo 24.5 gives its true longitude of Moon as Leo 23.19, at which place it is set into the figure of the heavens.

Neptune.—The longitude can be taken as at noon owing to its very slow motion. This is Taurus 9.21, retrograde.

Uranus.—Its longitude is at noon, namely, Virgo 8.52. It is seen to be retrograde and should be so marked in the map.

THE MAP OF THE HEAVENS.

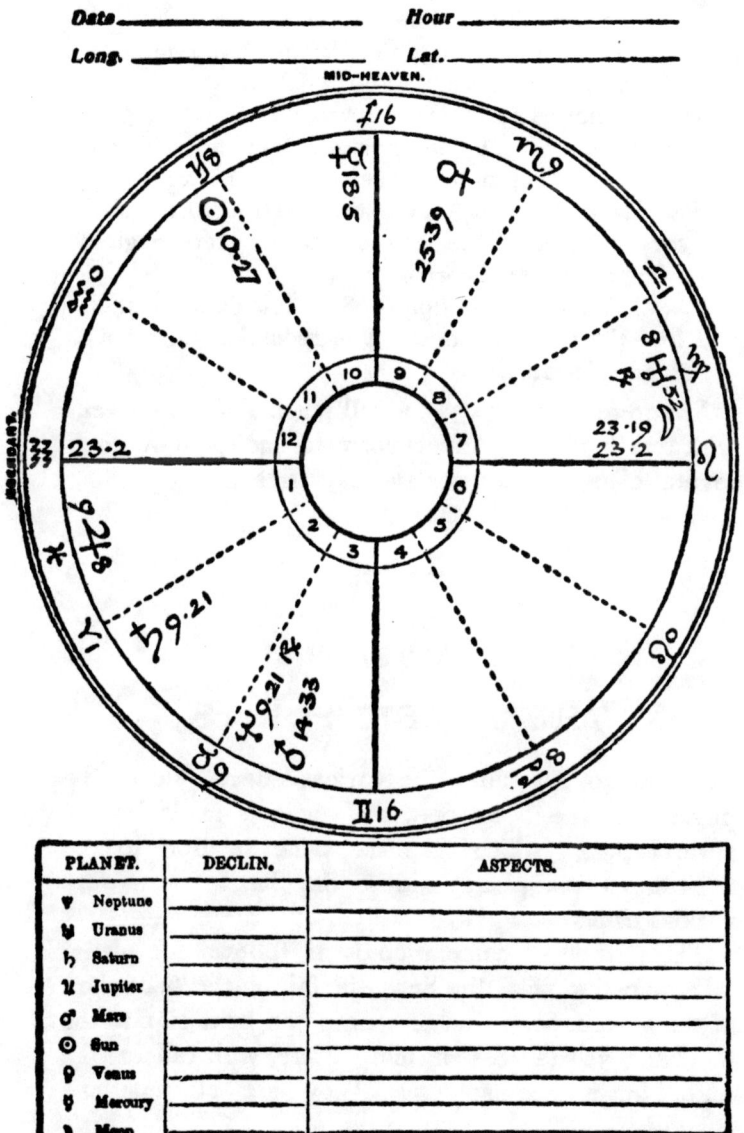

Saturn.—As at noon in Aries 9.21.

Jupiter.—Its motion of 12' per day gives 1' in 2 hours and its longitude is therefore Pisces 9.8.

Mars.—Its motion is 71' in 24 hours, and therefore 3' per hour. If we take 5' for equation it will be sufficiently near. Its longitude is thus reduced to Taurus 14.33.

Venus.—Its motion is 69' in one day and therefore about 4' for 1h. 30m. (time before noon). Its longitude when reduced is Scorpio 25.39.

Mercury.—Its diurnal motion is 68' at this date and therefore 4' for the equation. The reduction brings it to Sagittarius 18.5.

We present on page 33 the full scheme of the heavens with the Signs and Planets correctly indicated in their several places at the time and date given.

CHAPTER VII

THE ARABIC POINTS

In order to determine the various effects due to the planets in the horoscope, the ancients made use of several points which bore the same relation to the horizon as the planet did to the Sun. These were various named.

The method of calculation is as follows: A planet in conjunction with the Sun will fall on the Ascendant of the horoscope. One that is in the next sign to the Sun, and 30 degrees or more away, will fall in the 2nd House, and so on. They are all mundane points or places in the Houses regardless of their position in the signs of the zodiac.

Fortuna.—This is perhaps the best known of the many points, seeing that it is the only one that has survived in general use, owing no doubt to the fact that Ptolemy gives a place to it in his "Tetrabiblos, or Four Books on the Influence of the Stars," written in the second century A.D. Ptolemy makes it clear that the place of Fortuna is that held by the Moon at sunrise, and as it is a mundane position we are to understand equatorial sunrise. Thus, if the Moon was exactly at first quarter or 90 degrees from the Sun, the Moon would be on the lower meridian when the Sun was rising on the equator. At full Moon it would be exactly setting when the Sun was rising, and that would be the place of Fortuna.

This symbol represents property, land, houses, real estate, and possessions generally. It is called in the Chinese Tien (a field) and is represented by a circle with a cross enclosed within.

The Sword is the mundane position answering to the elongation of Mars. It it denoted by a scimitar with a cross handle. It denotes strife and contention, dangers, and powerful protections.

The Caduceus.—The staff of Mercury is represented by the Caduceus like two serpents on an upright staff, winged. It may be conveniently denoted by the figure 8, through which a straight sword is drawn. It indicates knowledge and the use of the faculties, with gain or loss thereby, according to the position in which it falls in conjunction or aspect to the planets.

The Heart is the symbol of Venus and is denoted

by a heart-shaped figure. It presides over the fortunes in domestic, social and love affairs.

The Pomegranate.—This is the symbol of Jupiter and denotes increase and expansion by those means represented by the House in which the symbol falls.

The Hour Glass is the symbol of Saturn or Chronos, the god of Time. He is the youngest of all the gods (planets), but comes to us as an old man bearing an hour-glass and a scythe. Wherever this symbol falls it denotes endurance and fidelity, security by lapse of time, gain by time contracts etc. But its aspects must be consulted, as in the case of all others.

To these ancient symbols I have added :—

The Lightning Flash.—The symbol of Uranus. It denotes genius and origination, invention and reforms. But if badly aspected or placed it shows destruction by force, sudden calamities, etc., as seen from the nature of Uranus. It is shown by a zig-zag line.

The Grille.—This symbol represents the planet Neptune. It is indicated by three lines crossed by three others. It denotes nebulosity, chaos, confusion, deception, intrigues, etc. It is a peculiar indication of a special class of intelligences, born in cycles of fifteen years, who are responsive to the higher vibrations of matter and sensitive to the appulsions of the finer forces in nature.

With all respect to the dictum of Ptolemy, as far as he is to be understood from translations which have come down to us through the Greek and Latin, I am disposed to think that inasmuch as we take the elongation of a planet by degrees of longitude, we ought to refer this elongation to the Ascendant of the horoscope

THE ARABIC POINTS

in degrees of longitude. This, at all events, agrees more exactly with my observations in regard to numerous horoscopes than the mundane position of the various symbols.

Referring these Points to the horoscope before us, we find the Sun to be distant from Aries 0 by ... ...
                                                       s. d. m.

	s.	d.	m.
Sun distant from Aries 0	9	10	31
The Moon from the same point is distant	4	23	19
Moon in advance of the Sun (subtract)	4	17	12
Place of Ascendant at birth	10	23	2
Remains longitude of Fortuna	6	5	50

Which is equivalent to Libra 5.50

Other positions being similarly taken, we have the figure of the heavens with the several points therein as on page 37.

CHAPTER VIII

JUDGING THE HOROSCOPE

THIS brings us to the essential part of Astrology, for up to the present moment we have been concerned largely with the construction of the horoscope, which is a purely astronomical process. It is when we begin to apply our astronomy to the affairs of life, and give it a human interpretation, that we too often part company with well-instructed if prejudiced people. However that may be, the facts are strongly in favour of Astrology, or at least of some degree of agreement between terrestrial conditions and celestial environment, which, so far as we are concerned, must in such case extend to ourselves collectively and individually.

With the horoscope before us, we at once see that it is significant of an Ishmaelite—one who runs contrary to the trend of the times and is liable to suffer thereby.

What suggests this is the presence of two malefic or inharmonious planets in the 3rd House in the sign Taurus opposed to Venus, and the Moon in opposition to the Ascendant. Then again, we find the two planets Uranus and Jupiter in opposition to one another, which certainly would not sustain any contracts or engagements into which he might enter with others, and the quadrature of the Sun to Saturn in the 2nd House points to financial loss. Mercury in the Midheaven makes of him a man of affairs and a public speaker. The remedial indication is the rising of Jupiter in sextile aspect to Neptune, and although it comports entirely with the grandiose schemes and projects which animate the mind of the man, and which bring him into touch with men of affluence and position, there is the danger that many of these fine bubbles will burst, for Uranus does not oppose Jupiter without endangering the fortunes through contracts (7th House) broken off or annulled.

In marital relations he cannot be regarded as fortunate, for the Moon is square to Venus, and Uranus (retrograde) is in the 7th House. This, at all events, is one of the unfortunate contracts to which reference has been made.

The rising of six planets in the horoscope, culminating in a weak Mercury, shows ambition and endeavour towards independence, and the Moon in trine to Mercury affords at least some indication of success in matters of publication or propaganda.

Referring now to the Arabic Points, we again find Uranus and Jupiter in opposition, while Mars and Neptune hold the lower angle of the horoscope. Except that these points are in good aspect to the rising Sun they would be highly dangerous to the life and fortunes. The Moon, which here indicates the place of Fortuna, is opposed to the radical Saturn (that is, Saturn's place in the radix or horoscope of birth), and Saturn is near that of Mars. There are, therefore, many elements of a discordant nature in this figure and yet his associations would have been helped considerably by the position of Venus (the Heart) in conjunction with the radical Sun, save that it is in square also to the radical Saturn.

The 4th House indicates the end of life, and here is affected by positions which seem to point to a violent and sudden and even a mysterious termination.

Now let us see what can be easily discovered about, this case from a rule of thumb judgment, based entirely on planetary positions in House. We know our planets and also what affairs are related to the various Houses. By a combination of these, aided by a modicum of intuition, we shall get very near to the truth about this case.

The 1st House rules the person and here holds the planet Jupiter. Jupiter shows increase and expansion. The person will be "expansive" and well developed, built entirely on the large side, full bodied, with a strong suggestion of the prosperous publican about him. So far we should be quite in order.

The 2nd House holds Saturn in the sign of its fall, Aries, and this planet is rendered the more harmful by its quadrature to the Sun. Hence, we should judge that Saturn would denude and impoverish the man, causing privation and periods of great adversity. This would be in line with the facts.

The 3rd House holds two malefic planets. Neptune tends to simulation, chicanery, fraud, misrepresentation, plots, etc. Mars denotes energy, enterprise, disputation, strife. The 3rd House rules collateral relatives and neighbours.

He never got on well with his brothers and early cut adrift. He was twice voted a nuisance as a neighbour and suffered loss through disputes.

The 7th House holds the Moon and Uranus retrograde. He married unfortunately (Moon square Venus), has courted publicity, is an energetic if illogical speaker, and has never been much in the confidence of his fellows. His claims to recognition are voted "worth backing." My own comment is that he banks too much on popular feeling and too little on solid fact.

The 9th House holds Venus in its fall. The attraction to a Southerner (Moon square Venus) may be regarded as one of the worst influences in his life. Instinct seems to tell him that long voyages and foreign parts are unfortunate to him, so perforce the foreign element has to be imported!

The 10th House holds Mercury in its fall. He has the talking faculty and can say well what he has in mind. But although he sways opinion he is short of a considered policy, and so fails from the fact that he has no definite objective and no straight line of direction.

The 11th House holds the Sun. This is squared by Saturn. He has friends and acquaintances and associates above his sphere in life, but they are more likely to pluck him in the end than to contribute anything to his advancement.

His aims are political. His methods indefinite and his policy a jungle of ill-favoured weeds.

Now, if we refer to the Arabic Points we find much confirmation. Jupiter in the 2nd House has given him money, but its opposition by Uranus shows bad contracts, alimony, and litigation. Moon square Venus, domestic troubles. Mars and Neptune in the 4th House, loss though dealing in real estate. Final adversity. Saturn in the 3rd House, distrust and jealousy among relations and neighbours.

We may now consider when events signified are likely to happen. This is effected by the process called "Direction."

CHAPTER IX

TIMING EVENTS

THE process of timing events is called "Direction." The points of the horoscope subject to direction or forward movement in the zodiac are :—

      The Midheaven,
      The Ascendant,
      The Sun,
      The Moon,
      Fortuna.

These are called "Significators." The planets to whose aspects and positions they are directed are called "Promittors," because they hold the promise or potency of whatever is signified.

The Midheaven is moved forward at the rate of one degree per year and the Ascendant is taken out under that Midheaven to which the direction reaches. The Sun, Moon, and Fortuna are similarly carried forward in the order of the signs at the rate of one degree for each year of life.

TIMING EVENTS

It is then seen that the Significators form aspects from time to time with the radical places of the planets, and all that has to be done is to note the number of degrees that are required to form the complete aspect, counting from the year of birth. The only possible mistake that can be made is in regard to the Ascendant. In this case you have merely to note the number of degrees which pass over the Midheaven in order to bring the Ascendant into aspect with a planet.

This calculation being made, you must then note the nature of the planet to which the Significator is directed, also the nature of affairs governed by the House in which the planet may be.

Lastly, you take note of the Significator which is directed. For the Sun and Midheaven have relation to the male sex and to affairs connected with the position, credit, honour, and standing. The Moon and Ascendant have relation to changes incidental to the environment, health, and general fortunes, while the Moon denotes female relations and the female sex generally.

As far as possible, interpretation should be made in terms of the environment and position of the subject whose horoscope is under consideration, and the potentialities of the birth horoscope should not be exceeded.

As an illustration of what is meant, we may cite the case of John Hemmings, who was born in the parish of St. Martin's, London, at the same time as King George III. When King George II died, John Hemmings lost his father and succeeded to his business, as the king did to his father's throne. But John was only an ironmonger. Nevertheless, he was married on the same day as the king and had the same issue, and fulfilled the portents of his horoscope by dying on the same day and at nearly the same hour as his sovereign lord.

It will thus be seen that the sphere of life into which a person is born, his environment at the time of a "direction," and the extent of his sphere of influence, have very much weight in the question as to what may or may not be predicted with certainty.

Applying these remarks to the case we have before us, it will be seen that the Moon is opposed to the Ascendant during the first year of life, and this would account for the death of the mother. The father having children by a former wife would account for the position of "ugly duckling" conferred upon the subject during infancy, and the sinister influence of planets in the 3rd House for many years afterwards.

Uranus coming to the opposition of the Ascendant about the same time as the rising of Jupiter, which takes place at six years of age, when the Midheaven will have moved forward 6 degrees to Sagittarius 22, coincided with the death of the grandfather and his removal to the home of his uncle. Here the 7th House denotes the grandfather and Uranus the separation by death. Jupiter appears to stand for the well disposed uncle in this case. By this transfer of interests the subject was temporarily benefited.

Now if we add 25 degrees to the Midheaven we come to the place of the Sun in Capricorn 10, and this has the square aspect of Saturn. At this time he lost his father and also his rightful share of the property, through the usurpation of his step-brothers.

Up to the outbreak of war he made considerable

progress, but like many another, he fell at the first ditch in the great obstacle race across France and was invalided home, and now, at the age of forty, has political ambitions under the ægis of the new democracy.

The best practice in "timing" is to be obtained from the horoscopes of those whose lives are well known to the student, and from whom much information can be gathered concerning the chief events at various times in the life.

CHAPTER X

TRANSITS

NEXT to Directions the influence of Transits is to be considered. Directions indicate the general nature of the period and enable us to predict the nature and source of good and ill effects in the life. Transits enable us to define the exact time at which those directions will come into play.

Everybody knows the history of the Great War. Most people know that the ex-Kaiser was born in Berlin, on the 27th January, 1859, at about three o'clock in the afternoon. Calculation has shown that the Midheaven was then in Pisces 21 degrees with Cancer 21 rising. The War Lord decided upon making his last great offensive at four o'clock in the morning, of the 21st March, 1918, by which movement he hoped to sweep the Allies into the sea. Unfortunately there was no astrologer on his staff to inform him that on that very day Mars was in exact opposition to the Midheaven of his horoscope, and Saturn close to the opposition of the Sun's place at his birth. It was a most unfortunate time at which to launch a great enterprise, and I take little credit to myself for having predicted the entire defeat of the German forces and the cessation of hostilities in November of the same year.

The directions operating at this time in the ex-Kaiser's horoscope were highly unfortunate, and his eventual downfall through his own allies was well defined by the opposition of Uranus to the Moon from the 11th House (allies), and the opposition of Saturn to the Sun at birth. Those who would study the directions operating in the sixtieth year of this remarkable life should look to Mars, the god of war, which held the Midheaven with Neptune in Pisces at the birth, and which in sixty years comes to the opposition of the Moon by direction. It was to this planet that the ex-Kaiser looked for his great achievement and glory. He staked everything on the power of the sword. Incidentally, we may note the position of Neptune in the sign Pisces as indicating the submarine campaign of unrestricted warfare. But it was this sword which was finally broken, and this murderous policy which arrayed the world against him. So his destiny was fulfilled by himself. Note also the arc of planets rising in the horoscope and culminating in the planet of chaos and confusion! Observe also the position of the Sun in its sign of fall (Aquarius) opposed by Saturn, also in its fall, and the Moon opposed by Uranus, which is elevated above it. The Sun has also the semisquare aspect of Neptune and

Mars, and rules the 2nd House, so that Saturn here in the 2nd, opposing an afflicted Sun indicated the entire loss of his dominions, while the afflicted Moon (ruler of the Ascendant) afflicted by Uranus showed a sudden downfall.

The positions of the Significators at birth are not the only ones that are capable of being affected by the transit of planets. The longitudes to which they are severally directed at any period of the life are equally vulnerable when affected by the transits of malefic planets, and equally productive of good effects when benefic planets are in transit over them. (See " Transits and Planetary Periods.")

Transits may be made by conjunction, opposition or aspect, and are to be regarded from the point of view of their radical House position when transiting a radical Significator, and from their directional position when transiting a "directional" place. Thus, the transit of Mars over the opposition of the Midheaven in the ex-Kaiser's horoscope at the end of August, 1914, was an adverse indication, which has to be referred to the radical position of Mars in the 10th House or Midheaven of the horoscope. It showed a false impulse and a political *faux pas*. But something more has to be said in reference to this transit, which gives it a significance above all other transits of the same sort—for obviously the planet had often passed over the same position in the horoscope.

The natures of the planets in transit over the Significators must of course always be the first point of consideration, and the radical position and aspects of the planet must be taken into account. For it is obvious that Jupiter will have little power for good if at birth he is badly placed and aspected. Similarly, Saturn would not dispose to heavy losses by his transit if at birth he was favourably aspecting the Significator over which he is in transit, and more especially if he was well aspected himself. Jupiter is not always one's fortunate planet or "lucky star." It may well be Saturn or another. Many people are disappointed of expected good by failing to take these facts into consideration.

Moreover, we must never forget that the planets, according to their several natures, always act in terms of ourselves and our environment. A man who is listless and without ambition will not make bold or successful enterprises under the transits of Mars. A man of small ideas will account himself lucky on the receipt of an unexpected dole. Great achievements can only come from great minds and high endeavours. Mars always exacts the penalty of a risk. Saturn demands time in which to mature his benefits. Jupiter is a planet of "great expectations" and oftentimes of little performance. Neptune dearly loves a plot or intrigue, and Uranus can make or break, according as a man is himself disposed to be constructive or destructive. Study yourself in relation to the celestial world about you. Man is an embodied universe. The planets are all compounded in his being. It is that which makes him responsive to their action.

Now let us look at another aspect of this interesting subject.

CHAPTER XI

THE INFLUENCE OF ECLIPSES

WHEN it is considered that a drop of twenty degrees of temperature, from 65 down to 45, has been registered in a quarter of an hour during an eclipse of the Sun in this country, it will not be thought remarkable that the ancients placed considerable value upon the nature of eclipses as portents. Physical effects have their mental and psychological reactions. So far as the physical effects of eclipses are concerned, it has been noted that the sudden fall of temperature during an eclipse of the Sun has resulted in an immediate uprush of heat from the interior of the earth in order to establish the equilibrium, with the result that such portions of the earth's surface as were unable to withstand the strain have been severely shaken and even broken up by earthquakes. Birds and beasts, responsive to environment, have gone to rest during the eclipse of the Sun at noon. A pale, sickly pallor has overcast the earth, and an unnatural stillness pervades the air, as if the whole world were waiting for something to happen. Then a strange thing occurs. You suddenly feel yourself lifted up, your feet are drawn forward from beneath you, and as suddenly drawn back again. The earth seems to flow beneath your feet, and with difficulty you maintain your equilibrium. It is an earth tremor. A little more and it would amount to an earthquake of a violent nature. As it is, however, buildings that are insecure rock and collapse. Trees wave ominously without the agency of the least breath of wind. Articles are thrown from their places within the house and the inmates momentarily clutch at the nearest support.

I remember that such an earthquake took place in India, and another of less force actually happened in the eastern counties of England. That is all I know about earthquakes from personal experience.

But there are on record, within modern times, some most disastrous results of eclipses. The eruption of Mont Pelée and the entire destruction of Martinique in the West Indies took place at the time of an eclipse which fell immediately overhead. The island of Krakatoa went down bodily into the sea, with 35,000 inhabitants, following an eclipse in the sign Taurus in conjunction with Neptune and Saturn.

The record of great earthquakes in connection with eclipses will be found more fully treated in my work, "Eclipses in Theory and Practice." It is enough, in this place, if one shows a physical dependence of the earth upon its celestial environment, and hence of individuals upon the same order of natural forces.

In considering eclipses in connection with the individual, it should be observed that eclipses of either luminary falling on the places of the Significators—the Sun, Moon, Midheaven and Ascendant—in a horoscope indicate adversity of some degree and nature. Falling on the Midheaven there is danger to the parents, and the head of the family usually suffers hurt or misfortune. Falling on the Sun's place in the horoscope, the father or (in case of a female) the husband is liable to dangerous sickness. On the place of the Moon, the mother and female relatives of mature age are shown as likely to be afflicted. On the Ascendant, the subject will himself be endangered. On Fortuna, there will be damage to or loss of estate and property. On the place of Venus, family and domestic affairs suffer, young females die or are afflicted with sickness. On the place of Mars, brothers are in danger. When falling on Uranus, grandparents or relatives of extreme age are indicated as liable to demise. On the place of Jupiter, uncles are afflicted. On the place of Mercury, aunts are similarly affected with sickness and misfortune.

The place in the horoscope where the eclipse falls should also be noted, as if in the 1st House the health may be undermined. If in the 2nd House, financial affairs are apt to take a bad turn, and so of the other Houses, according to their dominions and rulerships.

The times when dangers are likely to assail, as the result of adverse eclipse positions, may be known from the transits of the major planets, Neptune, Uranus, Saturn and Mars, over the place of the eclipse or its opposition. Events are thus oftentimes predicable to the exact date.

The law of compensation is, however, always at work, and although an eclipse falling on a Significator may bring death and disaster, there is always the possibility that the new set of conditions set up thereby may lead to brighter things in the near future. Thus, I have known an eclipse to fall on the place of the Sun in a horoscope, and in consequence the father has died and left a handsome fortune to his heirs, so that while nature hits hardly with one hand she soothes and compensates with the other. An eclipse falling on Jupiter in a horoscope is oftentimes beneficial through an immediate loss. But it must not be imagined that all eclipses are of evil significance. On the contrary, they may be harbingers of good. For if the eclipse takes place on a benefic planet, or one that is well aspected at birth, it will either pass without hurt or produce such changes as are to the immediate benefit of the individual.

The ephemeris will tell you when an eclipse is going to occur, whether it is one of the Sun or Moon, and where it will fall in the zodiac. In order to discover this you have only to notice where the New and Full Moons are formed. An eclipse of the Sun can only take place when there is a New Moon which falls within 18° 36′ of the Moon's node or its opposition. Thus, there was an eclipse of the Sun at the New Moon of October, 1920. The conjunction fell in Libra 20 and the Moon's node for that date was Scorpio 7.15, so that the Sun was only 17.15 from the node, but it could have been a mere contact and not a large eclipse. A more remarkable one is that of the Moon later in the same month, when the opposition was formed in the 4th degree of Taurus, the node being then in Scorpio 6.28 and its opposition in Taurus 6.28. The Full Moon was therefore totally eclipsed, being within 5 degrees of the node.

The transit of Mars has been mentioned in connection with the Spring offensive undertaken by the Germans in 1918. It was said that Mars was then in direct opposition to the Midheaven of the Kaiser's horoscope. It was also transiting the exact place of the eclipse of the Moon on March 12th, 1914, which has already been referred to as the portent of the Kaiser's downfall. For this eclipse was in opposition to the Midheaven of the horoscope. So we see that on the 31st July, 1914, when Mars was in transit over the place of this eclipse, the war was begun. Then on March 21st, 1918, when the final movement was made, Mars was again in the same longitude, Virgo 21.

By adding (1914-1859) 55 degrees to the Midheaven we come to Taurus 16, when the Ascendant is Leo 27.47. On August 21st, 1914, there was a large solar eclipse in Leo 27.34, and from that hour it was known that the war would last 4.25 years and end in the downfall of the Prussian autocrat.

CHAPTER XII

SIGNATURES OF THE PLANETS

EVERY planet has definite characteristics which impress themselves upon the child at birth. It may be due to the electrostatic condition of the atmosphere at the time of the child's first inspiration of air, by which a vital change takes place in the nature and determination of the blood. Or it may be due to some more occult process, of which as yet we have no certain knowledge. But whatever may be the active cause, it is certain that those who are born under the influence of a particular planet portray the characteristics of that planet most strongly in their mental temperament, and this finds reflection in both motive and action.

The planet which holds rule in the Midheaven at birth, or that which is rising, has chief influence in this matter. But should there be none either rising or setting or in the Midheaven, then we consult that which is strongest in the horoscope.

Thus, at the birth of the late Queen Victoria, Jupiter was in the Midheaven and the two luminaries were rising, the Sun, Moon, and Fortuna being in conjunction close to the Ascendant. These indications point to one of benevolent and august disposition, just and upright, but proud and regal, and of versatile intellect.

The Kaiser Wilhelm of Prussia had Neptune in the Midheaven conjoined with Mars. These planets point to subtlety, scheming, diplomacy, intrigue, usurpation, irascibility, fretfulness under restraint, impetuosity, violence. Acting together they are apt to generate more "steam" than the normal brain can accommodate, and the pressure thus set up would be apt to reveal itself by bursts of impulse and impetuosity, an unfortunate combination of influences in one who was autocratic head of so great an empire.

In the final estimate of the main characteristics one cannot go far wrong if he regards those planets which are in the plane of the horizon or meridian at the time of birth, but that which is nearest should have chief regard, for the nearer a planet may be to either of these great magnetic circles, the stronger will be the influence of that planet on the character and fortunes of the individual.

NEPTUNE

endows the subject with diplomatic faculty, insight,

intuitive perception of circumstance and character, detective powers, love of intrigue and scheming, a disposition to fiction, love for rhythmic movement. When afflicted, the planet shows a tendency to deception and cunning, prevarication, and marked unreliability. Well placed and aspected, there is often a degree of genius in the nature, and frequently a *penchant* for the violin or other stringed instrument.

URANUS

shows a strong but erratic character, one who is very wayward and self-opinionated, independent and impetuous. It gives faculty for engineering and construction generally. Those under its influence are usually inventive and original. They despise the beaten track and cut out a line in life for themselves. Their strongest powers are in evidence when they are opposed. They are argumentative and very critical. But when the planet is afflicted it indicates bigotry and stubbornness, and instead of being constructive the native is revolutionary, subversive and destructive, always running counter to the forces of law and order.

SATURN

disposes to a taciturn and melancholy habit of mind, or at least to a pensive and philosophical turn of thought, and its subjects are thrifty, careful, cautious and reticent. They are patient and enduring, and very steadfast in their affections, having rooted likes and dislikes. They are apt to become creatures of habit and lack flexibility of temperament. The poet, Dante Alghieri, whose works are tinged with a sombre philosophical melancholy, was born with Saturn rising in the sign Gemini in conjunction with Mercury and the Sun. Napoleon, the Man of Destiny, was born with Saturn in the Midheaven, and so was the ill-fated Napoleon III. When badly aspected, Saturn tends to produce a morbid and misanthropic person, of mean and covetous mind, tyrannous over the weak and poor, and wholly immersed in selfish thought and care.

JUPITER

renders the mind buoyant and hopeful, generous and just, incapable of lasting resentment, forgetful of injuries, disposed to ambitious projects on the grand scale, free, frank and easy-going, sympathetic and companionable. But when badly placed or aspected, Jupiter tends to exaggeration and extravagance, and lends itself to dissipation and high-living, bravado, bragging, and the complaint of the *nouveau riche* known as "swelled head." When not bragging to his compeers, this pompous type of Jovian is usually engaged in impressing his inferiors with the idea that the world is laid under tribute by the incident of his birth. Jupiter is at his best in all philanthropic work and organisation for the betterment of the race, whether as teacher, legislator, publisher, or prelate.

MARS

gives frankness, candour, directness of attack, incisiveness, courage, daring, warmth of feeling, and truthfulness. His faculty is executiveness. His sword is strength and his shield is fearlessness. But when badly aspected or placed, Mars tends to encourage disputation and quarrelling, strife and violence, destructiveness and lawlessness. Instead of industry we find thievishness and peculation, licentiousness and predatory instincts. The person is then careless of ways and means and only intent on present advantage, even if violence has to be employed. Mars makes either good sportsmen or great bullies, according to the nature of its aspects. When rising, the person is marked by a facial defect, a wart, mole, or scar. The poet Chaucer had a scar on the face and so had the Countess of Lovelace, daughter of the poet, Lord Byron. Both had Mars rising in the Ascendant.

The Sun

being in the Midheaven or Ascendant denotes a regal and magnanimous nature, clear-thinking, open-minded, frank, kindly, fond of the daylight and averse to obscurantism and cliques or cabals of all sorts, generous but firm and fit to govern and direct others.

When badly aspected, the Sun indicates a person who is fond of flattery and false praise, an egotist, an overbearing and self-regarding person, who is afflicted with in undue sense of his own importance, vain-glorious, fond of exaggeration and finery of all sorts, ruled by appearances rather than by intrinsic values. Weak and vacillating, unstable and time-serving.

Venus

renders the nature docile, gentle, kindly, suave, elegant, and artistic. The person is refined and cultured, sociably disposed and very amiable, so that many of the most esteemed leaders of society, of art and culture, are to be found among the scions of this planet.

The artistic sense to which Venus is allied may express itself variously in personal neatness and good taste, or in the production of works of art, music, painting, singing, sculpture, poetry, deportment, etc., according to its particular inflection, or it may merely dispose to an exquisite sense of the beautiful in art and nature. But when afflicted, this planet produces idleness, supineness, servility, disorder, uncleanness, and neglect of all the industries and obligations of social and domestic life. No planet is capable of greater perversion than Venus, and its position and aspects when rising or in the Midheaven have therefore to be carefully considered.

MERCURY

tends to activity, alertness, desire for knowledge, acuteness, watchfulness, general ability in languages and commerce, and often in science and art, the person being well informed and eager for knowledge of all sorts. They are quick and nimble, both physically and intellectually, and although not commanding the highest positions, being mostly too versatile and flexible, they are usually found in the van of all progressive movements. But when afflicted or weak, this planet disposes to pettiness and meanness of spirit, lack of ambition, and slavishness. Like Autolycus, afflicted or degenerate Mercurians are "pickers up of unconsidered trifles," mere scavengers and tale-bearers, busybodies, tattlers and mischief-makers, and frequently thieves.

THE MOON

exerts her benign influence in the direction of producing a character that is marked by grace and proper dignity, one who is kindly and humane, and very sympathetic, easily persuaded by appeal to the feelings, generous in the scorn of consequence, and well disposed according to the regulations of social and domestic life. The Lunar subjects are frequently disposed to public life and to activities which conduce to a degree of publicity. They are fond of travelling, have a disposition to romance, and are gifted with creative imagination in such sort that they may well figure as writers and artists. In effect they make their chief appeal to public sentiment and humane instincts, and by subserving the common need they frequently attain to fame and honours. But when afflicted, the Moon is representative of some of the most unfortunate and disreputable characteristics, and in this it is akin to the planet Venus, to which it is allied by nature. Such offspring of the Moon are dissolute and unsteady, given to licence and self-indulgence, wholly unstable and unreliable, shifty, wandering, drifting with the crowd and never finding anchorage.

These descriptions are of course partial. They may be greatly modified by the aspects of other planets as well as by sign-position, and there is of course the immense influence of environment and training to be taken into account. The normal and abnormal characteristics of each of the planets are here given, so that typal characters may be formed in the minds of students, with a view to selection of the ruling planet. Once this is found and the typal form of character defined, we have the key to any degree of service such knowledge may confer upon us in our dealings with others. Character and environment make up our earthly destiny, and if we would make the best of opportunity we must first know what Nature has fitted us to do. Time and season wait upon the man of purpose. It should not be thought that Astrology imports anything of fatalism into the problem of life. Fatality is only our name for ignorance of natural laws. A person is not vicious merely because he is born under the domination of a planet that is vitiated at his birth. Rather I should argue that he is so born because he is vicious. There is an affinity between character and environment, and the laws of life would appear to impel us to birth in an astral environment which is more or less nearly reflective of our inherent character. In this connection one may ponder with advantage the words of the Sage: "I am not good because I was born into an undefiled body; but being good, I was born into a body undefiled." And this, doubtless, puts the case, as I see it, as clearly as anything that has ever been written It is not the conditions of our earthly life that we have to deplore, but the weakness of human character which has allowed those conditions to continue so long without redress or reform. The purlieus of our great cities present a squalor that is both disgusting and reproachful, but what is more to be deplored is the fact that there are some content and even happy in such surroundings. No student of human nature can avoid the fact that environment is a reflex of mental condition. It is even so in the incident of birth.

CONCLUSION.

I HAVE now set out the foundation principles of the ancient science of Astrology. It is not to be regarded entirely in the light of a science so exact and dogmatic as chemistry or mathematics, but it will be difficult to escape the conclusion that its scope is so wide, and its points of contact so numerous, that some knowledge of other sciences becomes essential to the proper understanding and practice of Horoscopy. Thus, we cannot go far without some little knowledge of the mathematics and of astronomy. It will aid us greatly if we know something of physiology. In the working of foreign horoscopes, set for parts of the world distant from Greenwich, we have to assume some knowledge of geography. In collecting data from which to establish our observations we have recourse to history and biography.

No science is independent of others. Nothing and nobody exists for itself or himself alone. Astrology enforces and illustrates this interdependence of life more fully than most other sciences. And yet there is none that is more inclusive than the science of Astrology. It was the wisdom of the ancients. It will be the light of days to come.

All that I have said in these pages is of an elementary nature, designed to acquaint the reader with so much of the science as will enable him to prove its truth or falsity without regard to the opinions and prejudices of others, and to encourage the further study of the deeper problems of life and mind that are treated of in larger and more elaborate books than this. My readers will at least have the satisfaction of forming their own opinions of the subject in the light of this short exposition. If you want to know Astrology you must live with it and make it your own personal interest. But merely as a passing acquaintance it is not without its attractions for the average man of intelligence. If in the end you are able to say—I believe in Astrology, let me tell you that it has been said before, many times, in all climes and in all ages, and by some of the greatest intellects that ever graced the earth. You are in good company !

**CHARACTER READING
FROM HANDWRITING**

CONTENTS

CHAP.	PAGE
PREFACE	7
I. INTRODUCTION	9
II. GENERAL PRINCIPLES OF THE ART	11
III. NOTABLE EXAMPLES WITH DETAILED DELINEATIONS	24
IV. HANDWRITING COMPARED BY OCCUPATIONS	35
V. PRINCIPAL TRAITS OF CHARACTER	45
VI. HOW TO READ HANDWRITING	57

PREFACE

If it were necessary to make any excuse for the publication of this little book it would be that it has often been asked for. It is not a pretentious work : but just what it purports to be—a simple little guide to the art of character delineation from handwriting. In a small compass an endeavour has been made to give sufficient to interest, and, it is hoped, enough to instruct.

For the use of some of the signatures included here, and for some suggestions for the matter of the text, the present writer tenders his best thanks in acknowledgment to the Proprietors of the *Bazaar Exchange and Mart* newspaper, the owners of the copyright of Miss Rosa Baughan's " Character Indicated by Handwriting," and to the author.

If a more thorough and comprehensive treatment of the subject of Graphology is desired than could be given in a little book of this kind, the reader will be well advised to get a copy of Miss Baughan's book, which is published at 2*s.* 6*d*.

I
INTRODUCTION

THERE would be very few persons bold enough to deny that some indications of character may be gleaned from the study of handwriting. There are probably many others who would willingly agree that where the handwriting itself is clearly defined and possesses striking features, it may give an index to the character of the writer to some extent. Yet we are all in the habit of using the term "characteristic" when speaking of handwriting.

Even though we may express a doubt as to how far it may be possible to delineate character accurately from the handwriting, we know quite well that every person whose character is at all distinguished from the merely commonplace gives indications of this in every way: in mode of speech, in gesture, in clothes, in manner and, not least by any means, in the form and style of the handwriting.

The bold, ambitious, domineering individual carries himself differently to the plodding, persevering but humble and self-effacing one. We never have any doubt that the writing of these two persons is vastly dissimilar. The nervous, over-sensitive individual, with artistic tastes, is to be distinguished almost immediately from the callous, rough and rude person. Here, too, we have no doubt that a great difference will be shown in their handwritings. No two persons are alike in their characters ; no two write alike.

But as we can, and do, assort our acquaintances and friends into classes, though each differs somewhat from all the others, so various kinds of handwriting can be grouped and assorted. When we try to estimate the character of a person we have only one means of so doing. We compare him or her with others. Apart from comparison we can have no guide. All things are dependent upon this possibility of comparison. We know things only by their opposites.

This holds good in the case of handwriting. Every good quality that may be shown in the character of one handwriting is also expressed to the contrary in another. Character reading from handwriting is both a science and an art. It is a science in so far as it has collected examples of the handwriting of well-known persons, tabulated, classified and compared their writing to see how closely the character has been exemplified by it. From the numerous examples deductions have been drawn which form the practical laws of graphology.

Graphology is also an art, because the

application of these scientific laws or principles to examples of handwriting of persons whose character is unknown will reveal some indications of their principal temperamental points. This book will lay down those principles of the science by giving examples from well-known signatures. There can be no doubt at all in these cases. The autographs are given, and the characters of the writers are fairly well known. The various examples may be compared so that the points in common may be seen.

From these deductions general instructions will be given by which the more prominent characteristics of any handwriting may be ascertained and the character of the writer broadly delineated. This will be found a fascinating pastime in addition to affording an exercise for the practice of reasonable skill, easily to be obtained by a careful study of this little book.

II

GENERAL PRINCIPLES OF THE ART

It has been thought that because people are taught to write that the character or style of the handwriting depends entirely upon the school at which they were taught, or teacher by whom they were trained. The fallacy of this is at once apparent if we observe that no two pupils of the same master ever do write exactly alike. Even in early childhood, when we expect things to be said and done just as they are taught, we notice the differences that invariably occur.

However much skill on the part of the teacher is used, and however much perseverance is maintained on the part of the pupil, there is always a divergence from the copy. It must be remembered that in childhood the character is forming. It is in childhood, too, that the style of the handwriting is forming. The two grow up together as it were. No sooner does the child leave school and begin to develop indications of independent action than the handwriting itself leaves off at once, for good and all, the school style.

But as the character itself of the individual changes from year to year, not wholly or radically, of course, but in the way of modification in this direction and perhaps of expansion in the other, so too does the handwriting. Generally, however, the main features of the character remain to some extent fixed right through the life, altering only a little. So too, with the handwriting. After the character of the person has developed to maturity the style of the handwriting tends to fix. Both do vary, though, right through the life.

This is what we should expect. We should expect also to find that the handwriting varied with the exhibition of great emotional changes. This it does. When the lover dashes off, under the stress of a great passion, a letter to his love this will be found to reflect, in a measure, the crisis through which he is passing. When, too, a letter is penned in great grief it shows marks of it.

Those who possess the artistic temperament, with its outreach of imagination, and sympathy with the larger issues of life, will show this to be so in their handwriting. The quiet, contemplative habits of mind of the philosophizing individual with his more placid temperament will mark his handwriting. But as the artist may be subject, at times, to the same temperamental pressures, or absence of pressures as the philosopher, and as also the philosopher may feel the urge of a grand passion, both will tend in their handwriting style to merge, at those times, to a common mean.

It will be seen therefore that there is no royal road to success in the art of graphology. Like any other art it demands close attention and considerable study for accurate and detailed delineation. But, on the other hand, there are some very broad general principles which may be fairly easily mastered, and these enable one to give a broad idea of the character of the writer from a fairly simple study of it.

Here perhaps is the best place to give a word of warning. It is an old truism that extremes meet. This is very true of characteristics in handwriting. We are all able to distinguish quite easily between a pronounced virtue and an equally apparent vice. It must be remembered that a virtue if carried to too great a point may, and does, become a vice. For example, prudence is a great and becoming virtue. So, too, is caution. But carry these too far and the one may tend to become miserliness; the other suspicion. Frankness is a virtue. In excess it may prove very painful.

In handwriting we shall find these qualities reflected in every imaginable state and degree. It will need care, therefore, to see that a particular trait really means what it *seems* to mean. And each indication of character must be read in conjunction with the others, since these really modify the total character of the individual. Though this looks difficult it is not really so. In our intercourse with people the same thing happens. Certain peculiarities of temperament strike us first, but our impression of the character is modified as we learn to know the person better.

It will be found in these general principles that no apparent heed has been paid to the effect that the choice of a pen may have upon the character of the handwriting. For example, it will be suggested that from a thick handwriting certain indications may be gleaned. Yet it would seem that a person wrote thickly because a coarse or J-pen or quill is used. Herein lies one of the chief proofs of the truth of character delineation. The pen is chosen. It is chosen because it suits the hand. That means that the person who so uses it likes to produce that style of hand-

PRINCIPLES OF THE ART 15

writing, which is thus seen to be an indication of the temperament.

Paper which is used, too, also modifies the handwriting. And again we find that nearly every one finds out what best suits him, that which makes it easiest to write a suitable or characteristic hand, and this is adopted. We find, therefore, that all those things which we might at first sight consider would betray the handwriting and make it other than an indication of character, are actually points that help to strengthen the claims made for graphology as a science.

Race makes a difference in handwriting. The British write very differently from the French. The latter write differently from the Germans. But this also we ought to expect. For we realize that certain very broad indications of national character separate all these nations. One might go further and say that the English write differently from the Scots, the Welsh and Irish differently from either. This is so. But the differences are not perhaps so much marked as between British and French.

Louis de Bourbon

Again we find that some English people in their handwriting approach to a French style, just as some French approach the English. This we should expect to find since some

16 CHARACTER READING

English are very French in temperament, as some French are English in temperament. All these points will be dealt with later in more detail. Here we are concerned principally in laying down the bases of the science upon which graphology is founded.

Horatio Nelson

Perhaps the broadest general indication that is given by handwriting of any type or style is the tendency shown for the writing to ascend or descend in running across the page. The ascending style of handwriting usually indicates some measure of success or prosperity in the undertaking, because it is generally allied to those qualities which make such success possible and probable. Generally it is a mark of ambition and energy. It may be, of course, that such general indications may be contradicted by other features of the handwriting which would modify the success attained, but still mark the attempt at it.

Bonaparte

A handwriting, on the other hand, that shows a decided tendency to descend usually denotes the possession of the opposing qualities. There may possibly be ill-health with its consequent melancholy and disinclination to activity as the prevailing cause. Usually it means disappointment, failure, or at least non-success in life. In conjunction with other signs it may mean severe mental disturbance, pointing almost to insanity in some instances.

Marie Antoinette

In confirmation of the two general principles advanced above we may instance the signatures of famous generals and leaders. Their autographs almost invariably have the tendency to ascend, marking the fire and energy of their character. Illustrations are given later. As a typical example of the descending signature nothing could be more conclusive than that of the ill-starred Marie Antoinette at the termination of her career. Earlier examples, before the disasters of fate had separated her from husband and children and threatened her life, were ascendant, marking the earlier success of her career.

Generally speaking, it is not over-difficult to tell a man's handwriting from that of a woman's But it will be found that this difficulty increases with handwritings that deviate very much from the normal or sex styles. For example, those qualities which we regard as more particularly masculine have their reflection in the male handwriting, but when we get a woman who possesses those strong intellectual qualities which are usually attributed to the male sex, the handwriting will tend to become very masculine in character. Similarly, when a man shows those peculiar signs of temperament and disposition usually to be found in the ordinary woman, his handwriting will be seen to approach the feminine in style.

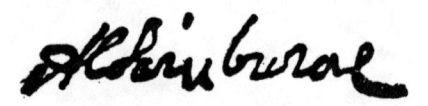

A heavy style of handwriting, that is one in which the whole of the line, both in upstrokes and downstrokes, tend to be thick, is usually indicative of sensuousness. It is generally accompanied by a love of beauty either in form or colour and is found to be typical of some painters, decorative artists, and great literary men and women. Imagination is often allied with this love of beauty. And though imagination is marked by other characteristics the handwriting of the imaginative individual is frequently conspicuous for this heavy style of line.

William Morris

The endings of words give valuable indications. The finals, as they are termed, may be either a light upstroke, a thick short one, an angular sweep, or almost no final at all. Each of these denotes something to the graphologist. When these finals are long, raised well up and rounded it is a sign of generosity. If instead of being raised the finals are long but take up space between the words it is an indication of prodigality. If the remainder of the handwriting indicates a lack of prudence the general effect would be that of extravagance leading almost to folly or even crime.

When the finals are less pronounced, stopping soon after turning up, it is a sign of economy. Carried to excess this indicates, when very little final at all is shown, avarice or miserliness. Finals that rise sharply, in an angular line, are indicative of quickness of temper, especially if the writing generally is of an ascendant character denoting ambition and energy. A softly rounded final indicates a gentleness of manner and a love of order and form. Finals, however, must be taken in conjunction with the general character of the handwriting, though they afford good indications by themselves.

Flourishes are a general indication of great value in determining the character. It may be said that the presence of a flourish beneath the signature is almost invariably an indication of love of admiration. It may err so grievously that it expresses merely inordinate vanity and senseless self-pride in the ordinary individual, though an elaborate flourish may

accompany a handwriting which otherwise indicates genius of outstanding character. The nature of the flourish itself must be taken to be largely modified by the general character of the handwriting.

As an example, we may suggest that a simple flourish, which is more nearly a bar only, indicates the love of admiration which is often found in the signatures of actresses and singers. Later many reproductions will be given to show how reliable a general indication this is.

Here we may well content ourselves with two signatures, one of the late Wilson Barrett, the actor, the other of the late Sims Reeves, the singer. In the former it is seen that the flourish is more a plain bar, which indicates also a self-assertiveness. In the latter the flourish is more elaborate, and the general character of the handwriting here indicates also sensuousness.

Handwriting that betrays between the letters a series of breaks is usually indicative of the mind of the dreamer, the visionary, allied with penetration and a rapid or intuitive judgment. The critical faculty is suggested here very considerably, though the form of the letters themselves will modify this general indication. On the other hand, a handwriting which runs on with words connected together, generally shows a rapidity of thought and sequence of ideas. A practical and synthetical mind, capable of organization and action, is thus suggested, rather than that of the analyst and critic.

A vertical, upright and hard handwriting may be considered a sign of a self-contained, self-sufficient and self-confident individuality. Selfishness is indicated by an angular upright style with short and angular terminals. Sloping hands generally denote sensitive and affectionate dispositions. Curved hands may be taken to show gentleness and tenderness, while those which are hard and angular, with a slope, indicate a lack of sentiment or romance and a general rectitude of disposition that regards the display of emotion as bad form and resents the slightest falling from grace : the letter of a puritanical mind.

An indication that must not be missed—it is, indeed, a very important one—is the crossing of the letter *t*. A plain, strong bar to the letter indicates a considerable degree of resoluteness and will-power. If the crossing is made high up and ascending it denotes a quick imperious temperament allied with strong will. The stroke to the *t* may be made in many and various ways, each of which possesses its peculiar significance. If the bar be high above the *t*, long and curved, it shows will, but without persistence. This might, indeed, almost be called wilfulness.

When the *t* bar, on the contrary, is very firm but with a tendency to descend, and is short and thick, this indicates a persistency of ideas with a very firm will-power. Placed high up on the letter it denotes an imperiousness of judgment and a despotism of power. When in addition to the firm crossing of the *t* in this fashion there is the bar beneath the signature tending to end in a heavier fashion than it begins, this emphasizes the power and self-assertiveness of the individual. The absence of the bar to the *t* is a sign of weakness of will.

Handwriting that tends to alter in size, with letters irregular, but running together in a good sequence, indicates imagination. Sometimes the capital letters in this type of handwriting are large and eccentric. The writing itself tends to become illegible. A distinction must be made, however, between the hand which becomes illegible because of the rapidity of thought of the writer and his attempt to transfer his thoughts to paper, and that of the mere illiterate. It must not be thought, however, that the writing of all imaginative persons has this character. It is often the case that it is not. But the characteristics given above, irregularity and large and eccentric capitals, are trustworthy indications of the imaginative faculty. The capital letters are generally well-marked, large and original in form.

III
NOTABLE EXAMPLES WITH DETAILED DELINEATIONS

No better method, it is thought, could be adopted in this book than to go on with some historic and notable examples of signatures. The full delineations of these will enable the student to see a practical application of the general principles given in the preceding section. It will also help him to acquire further knowledge of the art, as he sees how the complete delineation modifies, by emphasis or amplification or by neutralizing, some outstanding feature of the handwriting.

First of all then we will take the signature of Queen Victoria.

The boldness of the whole signature indicates a sense of real responsibility and power. The minute tendency to descend denotes the grief felt by the late sovereign for her many afflictions. The well-defined shapes of the capitals betray artistic feeling. The firmly crossed *t* denotes considerable will-power and energy. The angular form of the letters shows a degree of self-sufficiency not unmixed with a quickness of temper and a rigid obedience to the dictates of good form. The slope of the letters, and their formation, indicate much sympathy and tenderness, repressed somewhat by virtue of the official restraints imposed upon the expression of the personality.

Compare this signature with that of the famous Lord Protector Oliver Cromwell.

Here we have the boldness which betokens the sense of power and responsibility. But there the points of similarity end almost entirely. The whole handwriting tends to emphasize one feature—a hard, relentless nature which required neither sympathy nor support, nor gave either. The hand is extremely angular and upright. This denotes self-sufficiency and self-confidence. The angular terminals indicate selfishness. The will-power is indicated by the bar-like form of the *r* in the Christian name and by the downward bar given to the final double *l*. The signature shows at the finish the ascending tendency which marks ambition. Ruthless energy marks the whole handwriting.

Our next example presents once more very considerable differences. It is that of the Iron Duke.

What strikes one at first here is the strongly marked ascending movement of the signature. This denotes energy, ambition, and courage. It is difficult perhaps to say whether the Iron Duke was the more notorious for his energy or his courage. Certain it is that he was quite remarkable for both. The indomitable will-power is shown in the firm marking of the *t*. A sense of form, ability to organize, is shown by the shape of the initial *W*. The angularity of the handwriting denotes a measure of self-sufficiency and marked confidence. But the presence also of curves and a degree of slope indicates sympathy not altogether overridden. The high final indicates a generous and forgiving nature.

To pass now to a different class altogether we may take in turn Shakespeare, Byron, and the late Earl Beaconsfield.

In the signature of Shakespeare we shall find, as might have been expected, considerable originality, particularly in the surname. But even the Christian name is not without exceptional characteristics. Note, for example, the formation of the initial *W*. It is quite different

from almost any form of the letter ordinarily met with. It denotes much originality of conception. The gaps between the letters of the words shows intuitive grasp of character, which is also indicated in the surname in which gaps also occur. Both Christian and surname show a marked tendency to rise. This denotes ambition and energy.

The initial *S* and the curiously formed *h* and the graceful shape of the small *s*, in the centre of the surname, all indicate a mind of great power and imagination—differences in the sizes of the letters. The formation of the letters denote a perception of grace and beauty to be freely displayed, which we should anticipate in the poet who wrote Shakespeare's exquisite sonnets. It will be noted, too, that the character of the handwriting betrays many complex indications. We get upright strokes, self-sufficiency; with a tendency at times to roundness, sympathy and tenderness The long finals indicate almost the spendthrift in their form

A useful comparison may now be instituted between the above and the signature of Byron.

The ornate signature of Byron would lead us to suppose that his writings would display a tendency to fervidness and warmth. The general heaviness of the signature is an indication of sensuousness, modified considerably

in the upstrokes, as will be seen. Energy is marked by the ascending character of the autograph, and a degree of self-satisfaction by the angularity of some of the letters. The slope indicates a disposition affectionate and loving, and the rounding of some of the curves a tenderness not always in evidence. The long upturned final is a mark of great generosity. The gap between the letters indicates the capacity for observation and intuitive judgment; the well-designed capital a sense of form and a love of beauty. Some signatures of Byron have a flourish beneath them, indicating a greater measure of love of admiration.

One who was both statesman and littérateur was Benjamin Disraeli, and his signature might be anticipated to show some well-marked characteristics.

Here then are to be seen a complex of characters. Note the flourish beneath the name.

It is not of the ordinary straight-barred character. It is one that, turning in a graceful curve at both ends, marks artistic perception not unmixed with a love of recognition. The signature itself is slightly ascendant. Ambi-

tion and energy are typified. The highly original form of the letter *B* denotes pride, and the grasp for power is shown by the height of the capital letter in comparison with the remainder. The sequence of ideas and purpose is displayed by the perfectly formed letters running in easy movement from first to last and joined to the capital.

The final here, too, is not without its significance. It would tend to show a character in which there would be a disposition to quickness of temper modified by an ardent nature that wishes its own strength to be accepted without question. The slope of the letters and graceful form of them all, their softness and roundness, indicate a temperament in which suavity would vie with sympathy, relentlessness with tenderness. The hand of iron within the velvet glove perhaps best expresses this. There is withal an elegance and general form that are almost womanly in this hand, with the iron qualities of ambition and energy closely veiled.

Taking now a different type altogether we may present that of a great musician, Beethoven.

This is a signature that in boldness of execution is almost regal, without, however, the usual attributes of the holder of power and responsibility, plainness in the form of the letters. Here artistic form has run riot. Imagination, too, has fastened its sign manual upon the signature. Note the unusual style of the initial *B*. This may be compared almost with Shakespeare's *S* and *h*. The differing sizes of the letters also indicate imaginative genius. There is no flourish of any kind. Beethoven was too conscious of his own power to need any self-assertiveness or suggestion of love of recognition. The quality of his work left no necessity for it.

Tenderness is seen in the slope and roundness of the forms of some letters, but it is almost overcome by the fire of imagination and conception of form. The continuity of the letters suggests a sequence of ideas in the medium chosen for expression—creative activity rather than analysis of any kind.

NOTABLE EXAMPLES

Melancholy is indicated faintly by the tendency, just apparent, in the drooping of the signature.

Now we may turn to an example of a signature marked by an inordinate flourish.

Edgar Allan Poe

It was suggested before that a flourish usually indicates a love of applause, or is a sign of vanity. But the warning was given to read the flourish with the signature. Now the flourish of Edgar Allan Poe without a signature would indicate a very egotistical and vainglorious individual, though not unmarked with originality, as it has a definite form and is not a meaningless scrawl.

In conjunction with the signature of the famous American writer this receives striking corroboration. For here we see all the signs of imaginative power wedded to a melancholy that would result probably in work of a more or less morbid character. The initial letters are large and well-marked, characteristic of the imaginative thinker. The gaps between the letters and the words indicate critical faculty and intuition. The low barred finals denote an erratic temperament with irritability of disposition that may lead to insanity eventually. The upright form of the letters show the self-sufficiency and confidence of the egotist.

When we were detailing the general principles, a signature in which a general thickness predominated in the line was said to indicate sensuousness. Examples were given of the signature of William Morris and Algernon Swinburne. The difference between sensuousness and sensuality may be best shown by the illustration here of the signature of the great, but immoral, French tribune Mirabeau.

In the signatures both of Swinburne and Morris relief is afforded by some of the strokes and by the beauty of the form of Morris's writing. Mirabeau's signature has no such relief. It is heavy throughout. And this is the great distinction between the two. The emphatic stroke after the signature of Mirabeau, with the dot on either side and the upright character of the hand, all point to a selfishness and passionate self-worship that has little to redeem it except perhaps its strong individuality and sense of power

Compare Mirabeau again, for example, with Leighton.

NOTABLE EXAMPLES

It is seen at once how marvellous is the relief afforded by the form as well as the character of the signature. The bold dashes are portions of the initials, and the original shapes of these, together with the differing height of the letters, indicate a great deal of imaginative power.

[signature: Fred Leighton]

The bars show the sensuousness that decorate and glorify Leighton's paintings, but it is not carried to excess since the other parts of the signature are by comparison light. The bold cross to the *t* shows will, the light bar beneath the signature complacency, and a measure of self-satisfaction. The slopes and curves of the hand denote a tenderness and touch of the glamour of romance.

A peculiar type of handwriting, which is not an uncommon one, is that exhibited below.

[signature: David Livingstone]

The particular characteristic here is a persistency or obstinacy, which the possessors sometimes prefer to call determination, shown mostly by the peculiar downstrokes in conjunction with a style of handwriting that is nearly upright. The upright writing indicates self-satisfaction, the strongly barred *t* great will and the *g* without any return stroke emphasizes the possession of obstinacy or purpose: the determination not to be shaken from a purpose undertaken. In this instance—that of Livingstone—we get also tenderness in the curves of the letters, and a power of organization in the plainly defined form of the capital letters. It should be noted that the finals here indicate no prodigality, rather the reverse. The writer would guard and cherish his resources. There would be no wastefulness.

As an antithesis to the last we give here the signature of Crabbe the poet.

Geo Crabbe

Notice the difference in every respect between the two hands. Note the slope and the rounding of the letters, the upturned final, and the joining of the contraction of the first name to the surname. Here, then, we have the signs of a generous, tender nature, overflowing with the milk of human kindness. A sense of form is shown in the well-shaped capitals and a sequence of ideas and power of expression in the junction. Little imagination is indicated, nor is there anything assertive of self. It is a hand that indicates in excess feeling and sympathy for others.

IV

HANDWRITING COMPARED BY OCCUPATIONS

It might perhaps be thought that the occupation would tend to modify the character of the handwriting. In a measure perhaps this is true. But the individuals of any great class, of profession, for example, if they stand out of the ruck usually have very distinguishing traits. No two men or women are exactly alike. Their handwriting also varies. And this whether they be poets, musicians, scientists, lawyers, politicians, authors, editors, actors or actresses, painters, singers, or sculptors. There will be points of similarity whenever the temperament or disposition becomes identical. And when the characters are very much alike the handwritings will agree almost to identity.

For points of difference, first of all, in the actresses let us take the great Sarah Siddons and compare her with two other outstanding personalities, Lillie Langtry and Ellen Terry.

S Siddons

In this signature there are several very pronounced characteristics. The slope of the handwriting gives an idea of the extent of her sensitiveness, a capacity for realizing a part to such an extent that she became the personality she portrayed. Her audience, too, was quite carried away. Imaginative power is shown by the difference in the height of the letters. Intuition, a perception of ideas, is indicated most markedly by the breaks between the letters. Grace, of gesture, as an exposition of form, is shown in the shape of the capitals. There is no flourish.

Mrs. Langtry's signature is very different, but no less characteristic.

Sensuousness, the love of beauty, is shown in the bold outlines of heavy line. Imaginative power by the variation in the letters and original capitals. Artistic perception in the graceful forms of the letters. Will-power is betrayed by the heavy bar to the *t,* but the curve and height indicate less persistence with it. A dominating temperament is indicated by the heavy downstroke of the *y.* The flourish is almost a natural finish to such a signature, which indicates artistic capacity, but a love of recognition for it also.

The signature of Ellen Terry is also remarkable.

Imaginative power and artistic perception

are shown very strongly in the fine capitals and extreme sensuousness by the heaviness of the whole signature. Confidence of the most definite character in the uprightness of the letters, tenderness and kindness of heart by

[signature: Ellen Terry]

the rounded curves of the letters are also indicated. The strong bar beneath the signature, and the decision of the final *y*, with a final upturned, indicate generosity in addition to an imperious will.

For painters we might take as examples Rubens, Millais, and Watts.

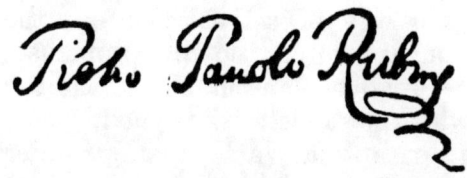

[signature: Pietro Paolo Rubens]

Here we get again sensuousness in the heavy outline and sense of beauty and form in the capitals. These latter follow more conventional lines and indicate less imagination than power of expression. Sensuousness is a predominant quality in most painters, and is seen in a marked degree amongst the great colourists. The curve of the whole signature suggests an ambition countered by melancholy. The form of the letters indicate a degree of tenderness. The tailed *R* and the final flourish an egotistical pride of achievement and love of recognition. There is little ideality about the signature of Rubens. He was a realist.

In Millais we have an entirely different type.

Ideality is denoted by the breaks in the second Christian name and in the surname. Imaginative power by the differing heights of the letters. Grace of form, keenly perceived and rendered, is suggested by the finely formed capitals. The slope of the letters denotes romanticism, and the line beneath the signature a measure of self-satisfaction, though neither an appeal for popular applause nor a mere egotistical flourish. It is the sign of a man who knows his work is good.

The autograph of Watts, again, is different though in some points resembling both of the two preceding.

The flourish here is indicative, by its doubled curve, of artistic perception rather than vanity, and the heavier signature sensuousness, the typical adjunct to the great colourist.

The precision of the whole signature indicates possession of the sense of detail; the strongly barred *t* will-power. The junction of the *W* to the letters of the surname denote sequence of ideas, and the forms of the capitals originality. The curves of the letters suggest a measure of sensitiveness and sympathy.

Amongst the great writers we will choose first of all three, from foreign countries, whose works are all of international reputation, viz. Zola, Tolstoy, and Mark Twain (S. L. Clemens). These we will follow up with three English writers.

To begin with Zola.

Here we are confronted with a bold and vigorous signature finished with just a trace of flourish, the sign here of power more than of vanity. The fairly heavy line of writing would suggest sensuousness; the fine and large capitals and some difference in the height of the letters imaginative capacity. But the great feature is gaps between capitals and small letters, and between the letters themselves. This is always an indication of the intuitive and penetrative mind, the analytical faculty, the necessary power for the realist. A slight descent would suggest morbidness.

The signature of Tolstoy is wholly different.

Leon. Tolstoy

Imaginative fire and perception of form is shown in the shape of the capitals and the bold flowing effect of the whole signature. Energy is indicated by the ascendant trend of the signature, a mark, too, of the optimism of Tolstoy's writing. Lucidity and sequence of ideas are denoted by the joining up of the letters wherever possible. The slope of the letters and their beautifully rounded curves indicate that tenderness of temperament, great sympathy and simplicity of manner that marked the great Russian writer.

In Mark Twain's signature there is little that resembles either of the other two.

Saml. L. Clemens

HANDWRITING COMPARED 41

In the flourish beneath the signature we have some evidence of the self-assertiveness of America's greatest humorist. The bold outline suggests a love of beauty, the well-formed capitals sense of form and some considerable originality. The definite final denotes willpower. The slope of the letters a degree of tenderness and a feeling for romance. The ascending signature shows energy and capacity.

For the English writers we will select Tennyson, Browning, and Thackeray.

Primarily the impression is that of sensuousness, from the thickness of the line, and ambition in the mounting of the signature. The capital letters are expressive also of an original and inventive mind. Tenderness and sentiment may be seen in the curves and in the slope of the letters, though both are considerably overborne by the rigidity of some of the strokes. Will is strongly marked in the definition of the *y* downstroke and in the final. In the junction of the whole signature there is indicated lucidity of expression.

In the signature of Robert Browning we perceive many differences from that of Tennyson.

The break in the surname indicates intuition

and deductive judgment. The clearly formed letters, regular shapes, and perfect alignment are indicative of the temperament and intellect

Robert Browning.

of the poet-philosopher. The slope and curve of the letters, much more apparent than in Tennyson and quite unmodified, speak of the fullest measure of tenderness and romanticism. The final letter *g*, larger than all the others, is an indication of frankness.

W. M. Thackeray.

This signature reveals at once the unresponsive and self-sufficient temperament that one would associate with a great satirist. Originality and inventiveness are displayed in the capitals. Extreme lucidity of ideas and power of expression in the junction of the whole signature. A slight descent is noticeable in the signature which would imply morbidness, possibly of outlook. The outstanding dot and the straight firm line beneath the signature denote first, attention to detail, and, secondly, the consciousness of work well done.

Differences will be immediately apparent

in musicians of such varying schools as those of Sullivan, Wagner, and Mendelssohn.

[signature: Arthur S. Sullivan]

How suggestive, for example, of sentiment, almost sentimentality, is the above. The shapes of the capitals denote sense of form, the flourish artistic perception, but the slope and rounded curves of the letters betray tenderness with dignity.

[signature: Richard Wagner]

Here there is a rugged grandeur, sensuousness, immense imagination, and a furore of expression. Note the dot—precision of detail, and the absence of flourish, save the soaring terminal of the r.

[signature: Felix Mendelssohn Bartholdy]

Artistic feeling, sentiment, grace of expression and tenderness almost to sweetness, well befitting the writer of "Lieder ohne Worte."

No less apparent will be the differences in

the three preachers: the Archbishop of Canterbury, the late C. H. Spurgeon, and the late Dr. Martineau.

Randall Winton:

This signature, written when Dr. Davidson was Bishop of Winchester, suggests the somewhat cold and chilling spirituality. The breaks in the signature the intuitive perception, the capitals imaginative power. Artistic perception is shown in the line beneath, tending to curve at either end.

C. H. Spurgeon

What a difference is here. A perfervid eloquence tinged with sensuousness, imagination, and romanticism is suggested by the heavier line, the dashing capitals, and general *movement* of the signature and its slope. The incisiveness of the final denotes a shrewd blow at the end of the perorations.

James Martineau

A plain, insistent, unimaginative but forceful personality. Mark the barring of the *t* and the firm dot to the *i*, the evenness of the whole signature, the open rounded curves, all expressive of will, peacefulness, and dignity.

V

PRINCIPAL TRAITS OF CHARACTER

From the foregoing it will have been seen how complex is the ordinary character and how many modifications are always present in the character itself and in the handwriting as an index to it. We cannot say of a man or of a woman, except it be in a very exceptional or almost impossible case, this person has such or such a quality and this is the character. However pronounced some characteristic may be there is nearly always something else that steps in to modify it.

It will be as well therefore here to give, with examples where possible, some of the principal traits of character that may readily be detected as outstanding features, to which reference will constantly be made in the subsequent section, "How to read character from handwriting."

Perhaps the best way to lay down a scheme of analysis of characteristics will be to formulate three classes: physical, intellectual, and moral. The divisions are necessarily somewhat arbitrary, since it is difficult to decide what are really physical characteristics and what are not. It is thought, however, that such a guide will be helpful to the student, and will make the book more easy of apprehension.

In the class of physical characteristics, as with the others for that matter, there will be seen to be almost an overlapping of some of the qualities, so fine is the distinction between them. But in conjunction with others they make a delineation much more accurate, because however much similarity there may appear there is no real identity. It is actually a case of secondary and tertiary colours, and so on into tones that all vary from one another, though they belong to the same general family.

To make reference easier each of the characteristics will be given an italic sub-head.

Physical Characteristics

Activity. Persons of a particularly active disposition usually write a fairly regular hand, medium to moderately thick line, strokes inclined to be upright, and a dash of movement about the signature with perhaps a tendency just apparent for it to rise along its length.

Ambition. An invariable sign of this is the constant rise in the whole of the signature. Ambition is usually present with a degree of self-assertion. It may be marked with imagination or originality, or not.

Calmness is generally marked by a plainness in the whole writing and a uniformity in the shape of the letters which tend to become open and round. Capitals are small and well made, and the line of the writing is even and firm.

Courage. This is usually associated with the signs of an ambitious temperament: a rising slope to lines of writing across the page, but marked with will and energy—which see. A typical signature is that of the heroic soldier, General Gordon.

Enthusiasm is a composite characteristic, and we may expect to find it in those who exhibit warmness of disposition, with energy and ambition. Enthusiasm is generally associated, too, with imagination. The enthusiastic person generally writes with a dash and fire, ascending line, flowing, easy capitals, well-barred *t*, and letters somewhat irregular and sloped.

Energy is usually distinguished in handwriting by angles rather than rounded curves, ascendant lines, with a low-barred *t* and very definitely defined downstrokes. Energy may be combined with ambition or not. It may be seen with or without imagination or intuition. It amplifies the possession of either of these qualities if present with them.

Indolence, as might be expected, gives the reverse impressions to the above. There is an absence of angles or decision in the strokes, which are represented by rather rounded, spineless and languid curves. The handwriting, in fact, suggests a writer who is too lazy to form the letters. This is particularly apparent towards the end of a word where the tendency is to develop into a scrawl. The difference between this and the writing of the impatient person is evident. In the latter case the writing is angular and impetuous in form.

Impulse is seen in a handwriting in which freedom of movement, angularity in form, and large capitals predominate. Downstrokes and upstrokes in *h* and *g* and *l* and *y*, for example, show this tendency to elongation, and rapidity of movement is betrayed by a slope and continuous joinings of letters and words.

Obstinacy will best be observed by turning to the example of the signature of David Livingstone. The handwriting, as a matter of course, conveys just that impression to the mind of the observer. It looks just what it is—the work of an individual who is perhaps long in coming to a conclusion, but having done so is not to be moved from it. How far removed, indeed, it is from the writing which betrays either imagination, activity, or even indolence.

Perseverance is a quality which is a compound of, or at least usually found in combination with, energy, patience, and will. The writing is usually angular rather than rounded, with straight and rigid lines across the page. Frequently there is an absence of imagination or originality—the capitals are therefore undistinguished in size or form. The *t* is well barred, punctuation is well marked, and the finals carried well forward but low down.

Intellectual Qualities

Caution. This is marked in a handwriting which often shows many other qualities also. It is rarely found as a predominant trait. Caution may be observed in a precision of detail in the writing. Most careful punctuation, usually a dash instead of, or in addition to, the normal stops. The writing is usually upright and compressed. Generally it shows little trace of imagination. Often it has the marks of intuition.

Imagination is often shown in the size and shape of the capitals—large and original in form. The handwriting as a whole often becomes nearly illegible owing to the rapidity of its execution in striving to keep pace with the thought of the writer. The letters are generally irregular in size—the most usual form is the tendency to angularity, but the writing of the imaginative individual is sometimes rounded, denoting tenderness.

Intuition is generally marked by letters which are disjointed in the signature. The angular form of letter is the usual in which intuition is most marked, as this form is indicative of energy and impulsiveness. Both these qualities are allied to the rapidity of thought processes associated with intuition.

But whereas the former two qualities may be normally suggestive of rapidity, without a laboured judgment and possibly therefore misdirection, on the other hand, intuition suggests quick penetrative and analytical capacity and correct judgment. In the one case the letters are connected—in the other, intuition, they are disconnected.

TRAITS OF CHARACTER

Judgment. When this is the result of deduction, a sequence of thought processes logically followed out, from the general to the particular, it is generally marked by a handwriting in which not only the letters, but even words themselves, are joined in a complete sequence. Compare, for instance, the signature which follows with that above.

In Gautier's work we have a marvellous power of observation and intuitive judgment shown in his writings. In Cuvier's formidable scientific judgments we have a sequence of ideas well illustrated in his joined signature and the flourish with which it terminates—this even forming an integral part of it.

Originality is usually displayed in the shapes of the capital letters, and indeed of the others also. It is as though the power of the mind controlled, as no doubt it does, the hand wielding the pen. There is no conscious striving after eccentricity of form. The latter is rather indicative of vanity. The person with marked originality forms his letters as he does because this best expresses his revolt against convention. The signature given below is a typical example.

Sensitiveness may be of two differing kinds. It may be the response to artistic feeling, or more nearly a moral characteristic, a sympathetic feeling for others. In both cases it is marked by a tendency to slope and curve in the letters. There is an absence of angularity and stiffness, and no self-assertiveness, upright characters or hardness in line and stroke, appears. The writing, like the character of the person, is softer, rounder, and more respondent to outside influences.

Versatility, like imagination, is marked by a difference in the height of the letters and by the peculiar forms of the latter, which tend to become spear-shaped in the loops. In the signature given below, that of a most versatile mind, it will be seen, too, that the characters are well formed, and not, as with the purely imaginative person, becoming illegible.

Will. Perhaps the best indication is that of the bar-like crossing of the *t*, and possibly a short bar beneath the signature. The down-

TRAITS OF CHARACTER

strokes are firm, and descending letters like *g* and *y* show this firm stroke very plainly. Will is generally associated with persons of energetic and self-assertive temperament, and the handwriting is therefore frequently of the angular type.

Moral Qualities

Amiability is best expressed by the slope and softly rounded curves of the handwriting, though it is often found in the more energetic types. Here the turns of the letters will be found rounded, while the hand maintains its general angularity. Tenderness, amiability in excess, is shown by the flowing curves and slope of the whole hand and capitals that conform to this general indication.

Florence A. Barclay

Candour is indicated by an open, rounded hand, of even quality, and generally straight across the page. There is a plainness and a frankness in the form of the letter which expresses this quality very obviously. It looks like the truth, the whole truth, and nothing but the truth—nothing to hide, nothing to display.

Conscientiousness follows much the same lines as candour. Punctuation is well marked, and there is an evidence of attention to detail throughout. Frequently the more brilliant intellectual qualities are missing from this type of hand, but in some cases, as in that of the signature given below, other fine qualities of the head as well as of the heart will be readily determined.

William T Stead.

Economy, which passes by almost insensible gradations into miserliness and avarice, is distinguished by the shortened finals of the letters and a general sense of carefulness in the formation of the letters themselves. The handwriting is usually of the angular type. There is no spreading out of this hand, broadcast over the paper, or large flowing initials. The whole handwriting indicates forethought and care. An exaggeration of these indications of carefulness show the gradation to avarice. Even the ascenders and descenders, in letters like *l* and *t* and *g* and *y* are shortened as though to avoid waste of ink and paper.

Generosity, as might be expected, reverses the indications above. Particularly is this seen in the case of the finals. These turn well up and round. The *y* final is allowed a broad spreading curve, and the capitals are of like proportions. Generosity is usually allied with tenderness, though not always so. When it is coupled with affection the hand is well sloped and curved.

Humility is betrayed by a small writing,

TRAITS OF CHARACTER

free from ostentation and flourish. A typical example, which shows also the analytical judgment of the great writer and didactic theologian, is that of Cardinal Newman.

Melancholy shows an exact reversal of ambition, and usually of energy also, in the descending character of the line of writing or signature. There is generally an absence of the typically selfish characteristics. The writing is more rounded, is inclined to the indolent and apathetic, though sometimes it may exhibit vitality and power. Its melancholy then becomes morbidness.

Pride is a quality that may run from justifiable self-satisfaction in high endeavour successfully completed to mere egotistical

parade. The usual signs in the handwriting are that of a large-sized letter with capitals that emphasize it. There will be generally a good form to these and probably a flourish beneath the signature. That of M. Guizot, given on page 55, is a good example.

Sensuousness. A typical adjunct to many painters and some writers. It is generally marked by the heaviness of the line of the signature. As was explained in the delineations of some of the great painters and writers, sensuousness, the love of beauty, must not be confused with its antithesis in excess, sensuality. In the latter the heaviness is unrelieved. In the former there is always some gradation in line strength.

Selfishness is indicated by angularity and compression of the handwriting. A rounded style of letter, although it may be compressed, is not an indication of selfishness. When the letter is very pronounced there is a tendency apparent in the initials to reverse the ordinary curve. Selfishness may also be indicated in a writing that is otherwise capable of showing affection, by the inversion of curve of capitals.

Tact is usually associated with a fine-lined handwriting, tending to the upright, but small and with spear-shaped loops to the *l* and *h*, a straightness of line and a final that extends without much rise to it.

Vanity is a quality that is easily identified in the ornate, and frequently otherwise unmeaning, flourish beneath the signature. The capitals, too, tend to exaggeration in form and over-elaboration. Perhaps we cannot do better, as some sort of a warning, to repeat here the signature of England's virgin Queen.

It must be remembered, however, that in the case of Elizabeth there were many brilliant qualities, which almost if not quite outset her abnormal vanity and love of admiration.

VI

HOW TO READ HANDWRITING

THE student will now have before him the elements of the science of graphology. It remains for him to apply these classified details as the art of reading character from handwriting. For this purpose some further general instructions are necessary and will be given here.

In making a reading from handwriting there are several processes to be executed, some of these are analytical, or breaking down processes, some synthetical, or building up, others are comparing and arranging processes.

58 CHARACTER READING

I have tried all sorts of manners to suspect about the North Pole - all ot manner. I can I think he also have but now shifts -

Prayer with uplift) arms Lost little sway O rustics, when you pray for fruit or grain.

He seems to me to want to made to venture to give him Guren angel, put or not in his ambitions; thereafter his life was a struggle

It should be quite obvious that to get a good reading more, very much more, than a simple signature is necessary. The reason for this is not far to seek. The signature, while it is usually very characteristic of the individual, does not, in itself, afford sufficient material for a careful and thorough delineation.

For a reading therefore to be of any real value a letter should be obtained if possible, and it is desirable that this should not be written for the specific purpose of the delineation. If the writer knows that what he is writing is to be subjected to analysis, dissection and criticism, he will almost inevitably attempt to write a formal hand, which will tend to disguise some or many of his characteristics.

A letter will not only afford a far greater amount of material for study, but it will allow the mind of the writer fair play to exhibit his leading characteristics. A few lines of writing will perhaps be done under the impulse of a single driving force and not give a chance for the interplay of forces. The letter, too, sometimes affords a quite legitimate further indication of the character of the writer by some of its subject-matter.

It will almost certainly be found that in a letter the writing itself varies during the progress of the communication. The writer lets himself go in time, and the ending, or latter part, probably gives the truest and best indications. But the beginnings and earlier parts are not without considerable value also. Here will be found, if they are to be found at all, hesitancy, caution, dissimulation, and many other negative qualities.

With the letter in front of him, then, the student should bend to his task. A preliminary survey will reveal whether the character of the writing as a whole is radically unaltered. This is a sign of extreme consistency, of course, if it be found present. A comparison may then be made between the signature and the body or text of the letter. Differences will nearly always be found here. The quality and quantity of such difference will mark the departure in extent from the high-water mark of consistency.

It will frequently be found that signs of some significance will be missing from one part of the letter and present in others. This merely betrays that reasonable failure in all-round consistency that is almost a virtue. Take, for example, generosity. Signs of this may be abundant in places yet almost wholly absent in others. This is an indication which

HOW TO READ HANDWRITING 61

will probably be found united to caution. It means that the individual while usually generous is not misled into mistaken generosity —he requires to be satisfied that the object upon which it is to be bestowed is worthy.

Many, if not all, of the other characteristics are subject to this same qualifying modification. If it were not so, graphology would

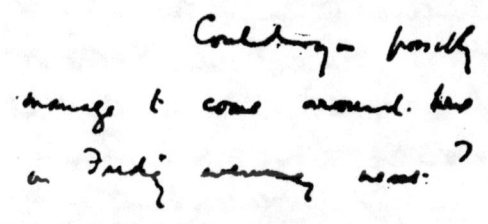

be of little service in determining character. For it is of the essence of psychology that our mental processes are complexes which will, and do, vary from moment to moment. Out of the strongest of them some more or less persistent course of action emerges. But this is always subject to deviation.

Character reading, then, is largely a question of balancing the indications after determining which these are. The dominants, the prevailing ones, are the most easily discerned. But the others must be closely sought for if the reading is to be really valuable.

It will be assumed that a fairly careful study has been made in the preceding chapters of the general principles, the detailed delineations, and then of the principal traits of character and how these may be recognized.

Analysis should then be made as follows: First ascertain the most significant factors. Is the writing upright or sloping, is it angular or rounded, compressed or open, regular in height, or irregular? Are the capitals large, unduly large, or normal? Do they follow more or less closely conventional forms,

[handwriting sample]

or are they original? Is the lining light or heavy? Are the downstrokes strongly marked or ordinarily so? Are the *t*'s strongly barred and at what height? Is the punctuation strong or deficient; of what character are the terminals, or finals of the letters? How are the loops made?

Each of these questions will be afforded an answer of some sort by the handwriting under study. And to each of them an indication of character is forthcoming from the previous matter of the book. The next process is comparison. Careful reference should be made to the examples to see how far they are identical in characteristic with that now to be resolved. Modifications will be constantly suggested by the comparisons,

HOW TO READ HANDWRITING

and these should be noted. Finally, the building-up process must begin. The various indications must be set off one against the other and a balance struck. The result will be a reasonable approximation to the character to be delineated.

It need hardly be said that practice and more practice is the key to success in character delineation from handwriting. Only those who are prepared to devote some little time and effort to it may expect to become expert in delineation. But even a simple reading of this book will, it is believed, be sufficient to show that there is much more in the art than meets the eye, and that many a pleasant hour may be spent in the study, and much amusement and entertainment given by the attempts to justify it.

Examples are given throughout the text of this section of handwritings of friends of the author. These will afford good material for study. No indications will be given of the identity of the hands individually, but it may be mentioned that one is an artist of no little repute, another a musician and composer, one a successful business man of considerable intellectual attainments, another a journalist, one a metaphysician, another an artist who has already achieved distinction, and finally a literary man of fine scholarship.

That the writer of the book may himself afford a problem for the reader as a final piece of illustration a few lines of the original MS. of this book are reproduced below.

FORTUNE TELLING BY NUMBERS

CONTENTS

CHAPTER	PAGE
INTRODUCTION	7
I. THE PROPERTIES OF NUMBERS	11
II. THE DAY-PLANET	19
III. THE HOUR-PLANET	26
IV. NAMES AND NUMBERS	35
V. THE MAGIC SQUARE	44
VI. PHONETIC VALUES	54

INTRODUCTION

ONE of the first things you will be told if you are seen reading this book will be that nobody—that is, no reasonable body—believes in mere Numbers having anything at all to do with the affairs of our daily life and thought. You will be told that these things belong to the superstition of bygone ages, and are only to be found in the twilight intelligence of the Oriental mind.

That is why the very enlightened Westerner will refuse to sit down with twelve others at a table, why he turns to the East in his religious observances, and never by any chance allows himself to light three cigarettes with the same match. He will deprive Nature of the last vestiges of symbolism rather than admit that there is any reason in the phrase—*Ex Oriente Lux*. Yet if by chance, by no means remote, he should happen to be a man of science, he will labour hard to prove to you that Nature is governed by laws, that dynamic and chemic forces are defined entirely by numerical ratios, and will convince you that all bodies have their definite laws of structure, and though he cannot tell you the reason why, he will show you micro-photographs which clearly prove his point. He will discourse at length upon the laws of the solar system, upon celestial mechanics and the law of periodicity, and the least suspicion of a doubt in your mind will be met with an avalanche of figures which will smother you into silence. You have only to express your own scepticism of his superior learning and he will go to great lengths in order to prove that Plato of the "twilight" period was right when he said: God geometrises.

That is the point at which I may take up the noon-day reasoner and tell him that when daylight began to dawn upon the Western world it was high noon in the Orient, and that his noon-day of intelligence will probably be the sunrise of some greater and more westerly development of the human mind. I would ask him whether Plato was not confirmed in his belief by Kepler, and whether Kepler was not demonstrably vindicated by Newton? But also I would ask him this question: When did God cease to geometrise?

But that immutability of the laws of Nature to which Science so fully subscribes is only another way of saying that Nature is the embodiment of a Supreme Intelligence. The ancients more humbly and simply affirmed that God said: " Let there be . . . and there was . . . and God saw that it was good." Such being the case we find ourselves all agreed that the universe is governed by numbers—that is, quantitative and qualitative relations expressed by figures—and we see also that as every human being is related to a universal environment and himself compounded of cosmic elements, the probability is that in sum and substance he answers to some mass chord of vibration which may quite simply be expressed as a definite colour, sound, or number. It may be called his ruling number. But whatever we call it there is very little doubt that it will play a most important part in his life and thought in relation to other units of life of the same or other number.

That is what we may learn in the course of our study of this subject, and it is that which I have here set out to prove in no uncertain manner. I shall be able to show, in effect, that not only are the fortunes of individuals reflected in the numerical circumstance of their births, their name-values and astral signatures, but that the same laws of enumeration by the art of the Kabalists may be applied with equal satisfactory results to the solution of other problems generally regarded as beyond the powers of the human mind to decide and therefore loosely referred to as chance happenings. I shall, in fine, attempt the demonstration of a numerical law of sequence in regard to mundane events which will go a long way to show, either that the course of events is necessarily predetermined by a law of correlated successiveness and so is exempt from human interference, or, as seems more logical and agreeable to the doctrine of human responsibility, that freedom of action in the individual is commensurate with his understanding of the laws imposed upon Nature and on the operations of human thought.

I shall hope to make my subject of interest to the general reader, and for that reason shall not further labour the argument than is necessary to carry point and conviction, preferring rather to make a plain statement of the facts and to leave them to speak for themselves. The conclusion to which they will inevitably point is that life and thought, instead of being a medley of chance happenings, a sort of lucky-bag in which every man is asked to have a dip at random, is in fact ordered by definite laws which collectively move by imperceptible degrees to a fixed and predetermined end.

Chapter I

THE PROPERTIES OF NUMBERS

Numbers are used to express quantitative values in relation to Unity, which of itself is the first expression of Zero. From Zero all numbers proceed and into Zero they all are resolved again. Thus it comes about that the digits from first to last are represented by the number 10, the Alpha and Omega of all enumeration. If we set out the digits in their order we find that they present to us a very curious set of relations, thus:

$$1 \quad 2 \quad 3 \quad 4 \quad 5 \quad 6 \quad 7 \quad 8 \quad 9.$$

Bringing the first and last of these series together in order successively, we have—

1 and 9 equals 10,
2 and 8 equals 10,
3 and 7 equals 10,
4 and 6 equals 10,

leaving behind the characteristic number 5, which is that representing the human species with its five avenues of sensation, its five digits or fingers, its five peduncles or toes, and its five great Races. This number was held in great veneration by the ancients, and we find that among the Chinese and among the Hindus there is a tendency to count by fives. Thus the Chinese have the Wu hing or five useful things, the five precepts of conduct, five ranks of office, five kinds of punishment, etc. The five useful things were clay, wood, metal, fire, and water.

> Saturn ruled earth or clay.
> Jupiter ruled wood.
> Venus ruled metal.
> Mars ruled fire.
> Mercury ruled water.

So they called the names of the planets the Earth Star, the Wood Star, the Metal Star, and so on. The five precepts were filial love, loyalty, marital fidelity, obedience, and sincerity, as regulating the relations between parents and their children, the rulers and the people, husbands and wives, masters and servants, man and friend. The five sorts of punishment were by fines, the rod, the scourge, banishment, and death.

Thus five may be said to stand for humanity and for human relations, man standing as it were in the middle ground of the manifest and unmanifest worlds, and in a measure cognising both the material and immaterial worlds by sense and thought, himself

THE PROPERTIES OF NUMBERS

being the embodiment of all, an epitome of the universe, a veritable microcosm.

> The total of the digits 1 to 9 is 45, or nine times 5.
> The total of the odd numbers is 25, or five times 5.
> The total of the even numbers is 20, or four times 5.

But each of the numbers comprised in the series has its traditional value as a symbol, thus:

One

is the symbol of the manifest Deity, who came forth from the Abyss of Nothingness, or Infinitude. It is the symbol of the Sun the light that shone in the darkness of the world's great night, and became the source of all revelation, of heat and light, of wisdom and love, the vortex centre of the universe of worlds, the archetype. Hence it is symbolised as a circle with a point in the centre. Thus: ⊙

Two

is the symbol of relativity, antithesis, witness, and confirmation. It denotes the binomial and "pairs of opposites," as positive and negative, active and passive, male and female, light and dark, etc., in relation to Unity, which stands for the first named of these, two standing for the second of them. It represents the dualism of manifested life, as God and Nature, Spirit and Matter, Osiris and Isis, and their interrelations. It denotes the Law of Alternation in natural operations. It embodies the idea of procreation, fruition, combination, relationship of opposites, the two conditions: manifest and unmanifest; the explicit and implicit; buying and selling. It is symbolised by the Moon.

Three

is the trilogy of Life, Substance, and Intelligence, applicable to the Divine BEING; of Force, Matter, and Consciousness, applicable to natural EXISTENCE. Creation, preservation, and resolution. Father, mother, and child—Osiris, Isis, and Horus—God, Nature, and Man. The three dimensions of space. The three postulates—thought, the thinker, and the thing. The three parts of Time—past, present, and future. Thus it denotes in itself the idea of extension in both time and space, and stands for penetration, procedure, and pervasion. It is symbolised by the planet Mars.

Four

is the number of reality and concretion. Solids, the cube or square, the cross. Physical laws, logic, reason. Appearance, physiognomy, science, cognition. Segmentation, partition, order, classification. The Wheel of Fortune, the Wheel of Ixion, the Wheel of the Law, sequence, enumeration. The intellect which discerns between the noumenal and

THE PROPERTIES OF NUMBERS

phenomenal, thought and perception. Discernment, discretion, relativity. It is symbolised by the planet Mercury.

FIVE

stands for inclusion, comprehension, understanding, judgment. Also for increase, fecundity, and propagation; and thus for self-expansion, the harvesting of the fruits of action, reward, equity, justice. Reproduction in the material world. Fatherhood, familism. By extension of self it becomes a symbol of sympathy, benevolence, charity, philanthropy, etc., and, by reflection, of joy, good fortune, and plenty. It is denoted by the planet Jupiter.

SIX

is the number of co-operation, of marriage, interlacing, link or connection. It represents the two triads in their interaction, the Seal of Solomon or interlaced triangles. The interplay of spirit and matter, the human soul; psychology, divination, communion, psychism, telepathy, psychometry, and alchemy. The Great Work. Co-ordination, concord, harmony, peace, satisfaction, happiness and material well-being. Intercourse and reciprocity. Connubiality, the relations of the sexes. It is indicated by the planet Venus.

Seven

is the number of Completion. Time and space. Duration and distance. Old age, decadence, and death, or endurance, stability, and immortality. The seven Ages, the seven days of the week, the seven Seals, the principles in man, notes and colours. The relations of the spiritual triad and the material cross or square. Evolution, wisdom, perfection, balance, rest and equity. It is symbolised by the planet Saturn.

Eight

is the number of dissolution, resolution; the cyclic law of periodicity. The breaking back of the natural to the spiritual, liberation, revolution, reaction, rupture, disintegration, segregation, decomposition, lesion, fracture, separation, expulsion, divorce. Also of inspiration, respiration, invention, genius. Deflection, loss, eccentricity, waywardness, refraction, aberration, and madness. It is symbolised by Uranus.

Nine

is the number of regeneration, the new life or birth of the spirit; spirituality, sense-extension, premonition, telepathy, going forth, voyaging. It denotes the dream state, clairvoyance, and clairaudience. Reformation, pulsation, rhythm; reaching out, extension, publication. Prophecy, prediction, revela-

THE PROPERTIES OF NUMBERS 17

tion; apparitions, spiritual perception, wraiths, mists, clouds, nebulæ, exile, obscuration. It is symbolised by Neptune.

The Cipher

stands for Eternity, immensity, the infinite, infinitude, space, the universe in concept, Divine conception, ideation, universality, circumambulation, navigation, circulation. Also for circumference, limitation, privation, restriction, and imperfection. Thus it is the universal paradox, the infinitely great and the infinitely small, Boundless Being and the Atom.

It will be seen that these ascriptions follow the order of the days of the week and the Hebraic system of planetary numbers, thus:

> 0 Space, 1 the Sun, 2 the Moon, 3 Mars, 4 Mercury, 5 Jupiter, 6 Venus, 7 Saturn, 8 Uranus, 9 Neptune (unknown to the ancients).

The corresponding days are 1 Sunday, 2 Monday, 3 Tuesday, 4 Wednesday, 5 Thursday, 6 Friday, 7 Saturday; 8 Uranus is the first of the new octave, the point of disruption; and 9 Neptune is the state of chaos, the nebula of the new order of existence. Astrologers affirm that Uranus is the octave of Mercury and Neptune that of Venus.

The days are called by the Hebrews: Yom (day)

18 FORTUNE TELLING BY NUMBERS

Echad (first, single, only), Sunday; yom Sheni (again, repetition, second, witness, change), Monday; yom Shelishi (a third, triple, a soldier of rank), Tuesday; yom Rebio'i (a fourth, intercourse, trade), Wednesday; yom Hamishi (the abdomen, a swelling, expansion), Thursday; yom Hashishi (a sixth, alabaster, fine linen, lily), Friday; yom Shebat (completion, a seventh, cessation, rest, end), Saturday. It is here seen that the names originally given to the numbers of the days are descriptive of the qualities and associations of the planets as defined by the science of Astrology. Let us now see what use we can make of the Planetary Numbers.

Chapter II

THE DAY-PLANET

The seven planets or celestial bodies (the Sun and Moon are thus regarded as planets from the point of view of the earth) correspond with the seven rays or colours of the spectrum or rainbow. These are:

Violet	—	Jupiter.
Indigo	—	Saturn.
Blue	—	Venus.
Green	—	Moon.
Yellow	—	Mercury.
Orange	—	Sun.
Red	—	Mars.

The Yellow ray is the most luminiferous or "light-carrying," and therefore corresponds with Mercury, which astrologically rules the intelligence principle by which we gain knowledge. Without light we should not know anything of colour, and what we knew of form would only extend to the narrow limits of the sense of touch. The Moon, as the earth's satellite, and in a recondite sense its nursery, corresponds to green. This is the predominant

20   FORTUNE TELLING BY NUMBERS

colour of the verdure and of the oceans of this planet. And because green is the most restful of all colours to terrestrial people, so red, the colour of Mars, is the most irritating and exciting, a "martial" colour truly, being the complementary colour to green.

Now just as there are seven planets and seven colours, so there are seven tones in a musical gamut. These again correspond to the planets, as—

> C to the Sun.
> D to Saturn.
> E to Mercury.
> F to the Moon.
> G to Mars.
> A to Venus.
> B to Jupiter.

And these seven colours, notes, and planets are all expressions of those seven principles in Nature which are called by ancients "the seven spirits," or Archangels, whose names are:

> Michael — the Sun.
> Gabriel — the Moon.
> Madimial — Mars.
> Raphael — Mercury.
> Zadkiel — Jupiter.
> Uriel — Venus.
> Samiel — Saturn.

From these correspondences we may know that there are seven types of human beings, each born under the dominant influence of a planetary ray, colour and tone. I am putting the case quite simply and without any scientific argument to uphold my statements, but if you think the matter out to its conclusion you will see that there are deep mysteries treading closely upon the heels of well-ascertained scientific facts, all going to show that all appearances in this world are simply due to vibrations. Possibly also, all forms of intelligence and all characters are but complex vibrations. But this is a matter which you must prove for yourself.

What I want to point out is that, in some intimate sense, a person born on a Monday is a different being to one who is born on a Tuesday, and that all those born on the same day of the week will display some dominant characteristic by which you may know them. This entails some little knowledge of the astrological natures of the planets, or of the types that are said to be born under them—that is, under their influence.

Number 1, The Sun (Sunday), gives a bright and cheerful disposition, a love of openness, frankness and truth. The person then born is confident and fearless, very candid and straightforward, magnanimous, loyal, generous and proud, jealous of honour and dignity. Such people account their good name as their greatest wealth, as defined by Shakespeare when he says:

"Who steals my purse, steals trash; 'tis something—nothing.
But he who robs me of my good name
Robs me of that which not enriches him,
But makes me poor indeed."

22 FORTUNE TELLING BY NUMBERS

Number 2, The Moon (Monday), gives less stability and firmness of disposition and character. Its subjects are variable, flexible, pliant and emotional. This variability and power of adaptation makes them suitable agents, representatives, public exponents, etc. They are fond of their homes and kindred, and are usually patriotic. Women born under the Moon are excellent mothers, and show unusual strength and tenacity of purpose in the rearing and defence of their offspring. Men born under the Moon are unstable and variable and seldom dependable. They are disposed to travelling and seafaring. Lunar people are remarkable dreamers, have vivid imaginative powers, and are romantic and impulsive.

Number 3, Mars (Tuesday), produces people of great executive powers, eager for conquest and exploration, capable in all pioneer work, ambitious, brave even to rashness, willing to take risks, great lovers of freedom, very zealous partizans, vehement, forceful, frank, outspoken and sincere. Women of Mars are usually very self-assertive and somewhat overbearing, desirous of rule, and frequently reckless as to ways and means. Men of Mars are found among all the great works of Vulcan, at the furnace, in the engine-room, on the battlefield, in the arsenal and factory, but also in the surgery and the chemical works.

Number 4, Mercury (Wednesday), gives an alert, quick, eager and attentive mind, apt in acquiring knowledges of all kinds, intelligent, good linguists, quick reckoners, capable handicraftsmen, adaptable, busy with many things and matters, men of affairs, usually very well informed, good business men. Traders and commercial men, merchants and shippers are to be found under the dominion of this planet. Women born under Mercury are generally active and nervous, fretful, querulous and talkative, and not the most comfortable to live with.

Number 5, Jupiter (Thursday), endows its natives with a kind, benevolent and generous disposition, but they are often self-indulgent, extravagant, and sometimes egotistical. When properly trained and educated they make good administrators, chancellors, judges, controllers, and directors. They are fond of good living, and of doing things generally upon the grand scale. When of small mind they are pompous and swell-headed. They are great producers, but also great consumers of knowledge and material. They are usually excellent managers and developers of other men's ideas. Women born under Jupiter are noted for their excellent dispositions and characters, and are chiefly remarkable for probity, industry, and goodness of heart.

Number 6, Venus (Friday), confers a light, joyous, and sometimes frivolous nature upon its subjects. They are generally neat, dainty, and well-groomed, but often gaudy and fanciful in their attire. They are disposed to the pursuit of social accomplishments and pleasures, music, singing, dancing, the fine arts, and the gentler crafts, such as weaving and spinning, embroidery and tapestry work, and sometimes to jewellery and perfumery. They are to be found among the artists, poets, musicians, actors, dealers in silks and fine linen, art fabrics, etc. In character they show flexibility, gentleness, refinement and politeness of manner, polish, style, and grace of deportment. But some are self-indulgent and ease-loving and lack force of character, relying on suavity and amiability to commend them to the world. While of great use to the world, since "all that is beautiful is useful," they are not essentially utilitarian.

Number 7, Saturn (Saturday), makes his subjects grave and severe. They are strict disciplinarians and deal harshly with themselves as well as others. They are sober, steadfast, patient, thrifty, careful, and are capable of becoming misanthropic and mean. They usually make a business of life and are often cynical and morose. They do not radiate much sunshine, nor do they seek it for themselves. They are born old in nature and are strangers to the joyousness of youth. They are generally earnest and thoughtful, and many of them are disposed to the study of philosophy and occultism and searching out the dark things of the spirit. But while thus philosophical when educated and refined, the lower types of Saturn are sordid and grubbing. They are always laborious and show an endless capacity for plodding, whether as speculative thinkers or merely sordid money-grubbers. Women born under Saturn are usually severe and sour-tempered, averse to marriage except for position and influence, and are generally unsympathetic and even tyrannous skinflints.

It will thus be seen that there are two very diverse types of subjects born under each of the planets. You may regard them as the mental and material expressions of the same principle. Education, training, and environment have very much to do with the particular expression of each character, for between these two extreme types there are many variants, and this will be seen to be due to the admixture of other planetary influences. Thus while the general type may be inferred from the day-planet, the particular expression of that type is to be known from the hour-planet, as defined in the next chapter.

CHAPTER III

THE HOUR-PLANET

The day begins at sunrise, which is at 6 o'clock in the morning at the equinox. This is the universal standard, and it has no regard to locality, so that at whatever place on the earth's surface a person may be born, the count of the hour is made from 6 o'clock in the morning.

There are six hours in each quarter, or quadrant, of the circle of the day, so that the first hour after sunrise is always ruled by the day-planet, or that which gives its name to the day, as the Sun on Sunday, Moon on Monday, etc. Then there are seven planets, and so the 1st, 8th, 15th, and 22nd hours after sunrise are ruled by the same planet in rotation. Thus on a Sunday we have—

SUN, 1st, 8th, 15th, 22nd hours.
Venus, 2nd, 9th, 16th, 23rd hours.
Mercury, 3rd, 10th, 17th, 24th hours.
Moon, 4th, 11th, 18th, 1st hour on **next day**, Monday.
Saturn, 5th, 12th, 19th, 2nd hour on next day.
Jupiter, 6th, 13th, 20th, 3rd hour on next day.
Mars, 7th, 14th, 21st, 4th hour on next day.

THE HOUR-PLANET

Thus, if a person was born at 3 o'clock in the afternoon of Sunday, the day-planet would be the Sun, and the hour-planet would be the 10th after sunrise, because there are six hours before noon and three afterwards expired up to the time of birth which takes place at the beginning of the 10th hour, and this we find to be ruled by Mercury on a Sunday, so the planets are the Sun and Mercury.

Now, in order to estimate the working value of these two planets in the life of the person, we have to find the product of their two numbers and reduce it to its unit or personal value. For in this scheme the day-planet denotes the spirit nature, the hour-planet the psychic nature, and their product is the physical nature. Thus we have spirit, soul, and body represented in the scheme of planetary interaction.

The Universal Numbers (distinct from the Hebraic referred to in Chapter I) are as follows:

Sun (morning) 1, (afternoon) 4.
Moon (morning) 7, (afternoon) 2.
Jupiter 3, Venus 6, Mars 9, Mercury 5, Saturn 8.

What is meant by morning and afternoon is this: from sunrise to noon is morning, and from noon to 6 p.m. is afternoon. Then from 6 p.m. to midnight is morning (on the other side of the earth), and from midnight to sunrise is afternoon (on the same side of

28 FORTUNE TELLING BY NUMBERS

the earth). The planetary numbers of the Sun and Moon are thus duplex, but the others are single. These numbers are traditional among the Kabalists. The following diagram shows the value of the Sun and Moon according to the time of birth:

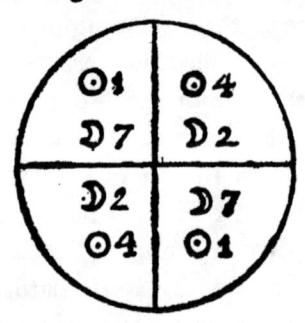

$$\begin{array}{c|c} \odot 1 & \odot 4 \\ \mathcal{D} 7 & \mathcal{D} 2 \\ \hline \mathcal{D} 2 & \mathcal{D} 7 \\ \odot 4 & \odot 1 \end{array}$$

We have seen that the person born on Sunday at 3 p.m. was under the day-planet of Sun, and as the time was afternoon it has the negative value of 4. Then we found that the planet was Mercury, whose number is 5. If, therefore, we multiply 4 by 5 we get 20, which being reduced to its unit value 2 plus 0 gives 2, which is the negative Moon number, and so we know that the final expression of the individuality at that time and on that day is the personal form of the negative Moon. The character and fortune of the person will therefore be of the negative lunar nature, not forceful, but very pliant and easily swayed, rather indolent, and subject to many mutations—a "doormat" liable to be subjugated by the will of other and more virile persons and frequently imposed

THE HOUR-PLANET

upon, leading an unsettled and changeful life, with ill-defined projects and very little power of self-direction and control; emotional and sensitive.

You will see that these delineations require some astrological knowledge, and there are many books at your disposal for gaining this knowledge in an inexpensive way. You will find them all given in my "Astrology." But I may here say that all the best, most effective and active qualities of the planets are derived from their positive vibrations, and the less distinguished ones from the negative numbers or vibrations.

In order to make the study of this subject as easy as possible to those who are apt to lose their way in calculations of this sort, I produce on pp. 30 and 31 a table of the planetary hours for each day of the week.

This Table of the Planetary Hours shows the planet ruling at the beginning of any hour of the day or night, and whether the hour is positive or negative. It also shows how the day-planet, which gives its name to the first hour each day of the week at 6 o'clock in the morning, is derived by regular rotation from any starting-point. Thus there are seven planets, and after three revolutions of 21 hours there are three more hours needed to complete the day of 24 hours, and the fourth hour will always be that planet which rules the first hour of the next day and gives its name to the day. This shows why the days

Time.	P. or N.	Sun.	Mon.	Tues.	Wed.	Thurs.	Fri.	Sat.
6 a.m.	Pos.	Sun.	Moon.	Mars.	Mercury.	Jupiter.	Venus.	Saturn.
7 "	"	Venus.	Saturn.	Sun.	Moon.	Mars.	Mercury.	Jupiter.
8 "	"	Mercury.	Jupiter.	Venus.	Saturn.	Sun.	Moon.	Mars.
9 "	"	Moon.	Mars.	Mercury.	Jupiter.	Venus.	Saturn.	Sun.
10 "	"	Saturn.	Sun.	Moon.	Mars.	Mercury.	Jupiter.	Venus.
11 "	"	Jupiter.	Venus.	Saturn.	Sun.	Moon.	Mars.	Mercury.
Noon.	Neg.	Mars.	Mercury.	Jupiter.	Venus.	Saturn.	Sun.	Moon.
1 p.m.	"	Sun.	Moon.	Mars.	Mercury.	Jupiter.	Venus.	Saturn.
2 "	"	Venus.	Saturn.	Sun.	Moon.	Mars.	Mercury.	Jupiter.
3 "	"	Mercury.	Jupiter.	Venus.	Saturn.	Sun.	Moon.	Mars.
4 "	"	Moon.	Mars.	Mercury.	Jupiter.	Venus.	Saturn.	Sun.
5 "	"	Saturn.	Sun.	Moon.	Mars.	Mercury.	Jupiter.	Venus.

THE HOUR-PLANET

6 p.m.	Pos.	Jupiter.	Venus.	Saturn.	Sun.	Moon.	Mars.	Mercury.
7 ,,	,,	Mars.	Mercury.	Jupiter.	Venus.	Saturn.	Sun.	Moon.
8 ,,	,,	Sun.	Moon.	Mars.	Mercury.	Jupiter.	Venus.	Saturn.
9 ,,	,,	Venus.	Saturn.	Sun.	Moon.	Mars.	Mercury.	Jupiter.
10 ,,	,,	Mercury.	Jupiter.	Venus.	Saturn.	Sun.	Moon.	Mars.
11 ,,	,,	Moon.	Mars.	Mercury.	Jupiter.	Venus.	Saturn.	Sun.
Midnight.	Neg.	Saturn.	Sun.	Moon.	Mars.	Mercury.	Jupiter.	Venus.
1 a.m.	,,	Jupiter.	Venus.	Saturn.	Sun.	Moon.	Mars.	Mercury.
2 ,,	,,	Mars.	Mercury.	Jupiter.	Venus.	Saturn.	Sun.	Moon.
3 ,,	,,	Sun.	Moon.	Mars.	Mercury.	Jupiter.	Venus.	Saturn.
4 ,,	,,	Venus.	Saturn.	Sun.	Moon.	Mars.	Mercury.	Jupiter.
5 ,,	,,	Mercury.	Jupiter.	Venus.	Saturn.	Sun.	Moon.	Mars.

are called by their respective names which are universally the same, and why there are only seven days to the week.

Therefore if a person is born on a Tuesday at 1 o'clock, or between 1 and 2 o'clock in the afternoon, he would come under the day-planet of Mars and the hour-planet of Mars also, and would be a singularly virile and forceful person, with strong martial and athletic tendencies and a considerable degree of ambition. If a woman is born at this time she is self-reliant, independent, forceful, and sometimes self-assertive, with a fondness for the more masculine pursuits of life and usually a great lover of outdoor sports. So you may judge concerning the other days and hours throughout the week. But in order to know the final expression of the individual character through the physical personality, you must multiply the two numbers of the day and hour planets together and reduce them to the unit value, and then you have the individual as he appears on the physical plane of life. Character, which plays so great a part in the formation of destiny, is thus seen to be the expression of the individual as seen through the coloured glass of personality. It is as Thackeray says: "You sow an act and reap a habit; you sow a habit and reap a character; you sow a character and reap a destiny." This is why the knowledge of character becomes of such great importance.

But each colour, number, or tone is in reality a

synthesis of all the other colours, numbers, etc., only that which is dominant is externally manifested. We call a body red or green because it appears so. We are all compounded of cosmic elements, but one element in us dominates the rest, and so gives us a distinctive character. Thus one person has Saturn strongest in his composition, or rather most active. It is the active principle in everybody which determines his character. This is well understood by students of chemistry. Nature is the Great Alchemist. A person under Jupiter will have for his colour Violet. This will be his ray. But Violet is not his only colour, it is merely his dominant or active colour or principle. He is not always Jovian, though naturally so by temperament. Sometimes he is very forceful and violent. That is when the Red or Mars principle gets the upper hand in him. At other times he is morose and depressed and melancholy. That is when the Indigo or Saturn principle gets the upper hand. And so we see that Violet takes something of the Red and something of the Indigo into its composition, and out of two very distinct and opposing elements it produces a third which is unlike either. If you bend the spectrum round so as to bring the two ends of the colour scale together, you will find that Red is on the one side of Violet and that Indigo is on the other side of it. But Red is only intensified Orange, which again is only intensified Yellow, as if the Sun's rays had been brought to a focus, and from being scarcely hot they come to burn intensely. Similarly Indigo is only intensified Blue, and Blue and Yellow make Green. In a peculiar sense, therefore, Green is the dominant colour of our earth's colour scheme. The characteristics corresponding to this colour are those which control the vast majority of our humanity. The Moon thus becomes a symbol of the people.

Taking this idea of character as the implicit cause of all destiny and variation of fortune, let us see what can be found of interest in the use of Numbers as regards our general fortunes.

Chapter IV

NAMES AND NUMBERS

If you want to know the numerical value of your name and its working power in the world, you must take out from the following Table your name-value, letter by letter, using your full Christian and Surname, or your pen-name if an author, or your trade-name if in business, and add them together, reduce them to unit value, and so get a single figure ranging from 1 to 9.

This must be done under the Sun and also under the Moon, and the result will give the earth-name expressed in Number.

Suppose, for instance, that I want the value of my own pen-name Sepharial. Along the line of the Sun I take out the values S8, E3, P6, H3, A1, R3, I9, A1, L5, which gives when added, 39 or 3.

Then from the Moon line I take out the figures: S3, E9, P5, H8, A7, R9, I3, A7, L6, which amount in all to 57 or 3.

These have to be multiplied together and reduced to unit value—namely, 3 times 3, which gives 9 as the unit. The two Jovian numbers 3 expressed as 9 show a strongly optimistic nature expressed as executive fighting force, a Crusader in fact.

Here is the table of Name-Values:

Sun	1	5	6	9	3	8	8	3	9	6	5	7
	A	B	C	D	E	F	G	H	IJ	K	L	M
	N	O	P	Q	R	S	T	U	VW	X	Y	Z
Moon	7	1	5	6	9	3	8	8	3	9	6	5

But in the case of a person using only his or her own name the full Christian and Surname must be taken out along the Sun line and also along the Moon line, and each line must be reduced to unit value by successively adding together the figures contained in it, until only one remains. Then the two lines or unit values of those lines must be multiplied together, and the number thus obtained must again be reduced to unit value. This will be the working value of the name on the material plane of action and will show the destiny of the person.

But all persons are not equally fortunate at one and the same time, as appears from the fact that one man's gain is another's loss, and none has equal fortune at all times alike, so that we are led to inquire what may be the controlling factor. This will be found on experiment to rest in the agreement or disagreement of the planetary-hour with the name-value of a person, so that if one has the name-value of 6 derived from the Sun and Moon lines he must commence all important affairs in the positive hour of Venus or the negative hour of Jupiter.

If his name-value should be 7, which is the positive Moon number, he must operate in the hour of the Moon in the morning or the evening and disregard the hours of the Moon in the afternoon and night, because these are negative. But particularly he must avoid the hours of Mars and Saturn, for they are directly opposed to his interests. Thus all men may work to the best effect by following the wisdom of Solomon the King, who said: " There is a time for everything and a season for every purpose under the heavens."

Similarly a person may reinforce his working value by adopting such colours as correspond with his own name-value. These colours have already been associated with the seven planets and also with the numbers attached to the planets, so that they need not be repeated here.

Also by choosing a house whose number is either his own unit name-value or a multiple whose unit value is the same as his own, much strength is added to the working power of the individual.

The most powerful alliances, the best assorted marriages, and the most successful working partnerships, are derived from the combination of two units, whose sum is equal to 10.

Thus a man whose value is 6 should wed with a women whose value is 4, and *vice versa*. One whose value is 5 should wed with a 5. One whose value is 3 should wed with a 7. A man whose value is 9 should wed a woman whose value is 1.

The reason for this is, that the numbers 1 and 0 are the indicative of the primary positive and negative forces in the universe, which we call crudely male and female, because they ultimate as such in regard to sex. But there are women whose minds are far more masculine and virile than those of men, and men whose minds are more conceptual and passive than those of many women. But since the universe is founded on order and number, we come into relations with Nature more nearly when acceding to her laws of operation. But where we cannot supplement our defects we can at least harmonise our natures by due selection of those units with whom we have to come into closest contact from day to day. By harmonising ourselves with Nature we have tremendous forces always playing in the same direction as the individual will, and thus the best working conditions are obtained for all.

So that if any would use the planetary-values in connection with their own name-values, let them begin all important operations in their own planetary-hour, using the positive hour in the morning and evening and the negative hour in the afternoon or night. Morning in this sense is from 6 a.m. to noon. Afternoon is from noon to 6 p.m. Evening is from 6 p.m. to midnight, and night is from midnight to 6 a.m., when the new day begins.

To strengthen the effect one's own day and hour should be employed on a day when the ruling planet is well aspected by the planet to be employed. This entails some little knowledge of Astrology, but not so much as need trouble anybody not disposed to a thorough study of that fascinating subject.

Another most excellent method of assuring success is to take the day-planet number and the hour-planet number, and add them together. If they are the same as your own name-number you will have great success in everything you undertake at the time—that is, during the said planetary-hour. But you will also be successful if your name-number is the same as that produced from the day and hour planets when multiplied together.

Thus if your name-number is 6 and the day is Saturday 8, and the hour Jupiter 3, the two added together make 11 or 2, and this is not the same as 6, but when multipled we get 8 times 3, and these make 24 or 6, so that it is the time for increasing one's efforts and pushing one's affairs.

We may now take some of the more general indications of the fortunes of an individual to be derived from Numbers. One of these is to be found in the famous Pyramid of Fortune. To build this you have to write your question on a sheet of paper thus; for example:

   Shall I gain my wish?

There are five words in this question, and they contain five, one, four, two, and four letters, respectively. The more words you use the more trouble you will have to get at the answer. The ancients were very wise.

 Well, then, we have to set down the figures—

$$5\ 5\ 1\ 4\ 2\ 4,$$

and whenever there are more than nine letters in a word, or more than 9 words in a sentence, you must reject nine and take the remainder. Now add together the first and second figures of the line, and when they amount to more than nine, reject nine and put down the remainder. Thus 5 and 5 are ten, and so we put down 1 under the two figures, then we take the second figure which is 5, and add it to the third figure which is 1, and put down 6 below the two figures added together. In effect, after doing this all through the line of figures, we get a second row, thus:

$$\begin{array}{c}5\ 5\ 1\ 4\ 2\ 4\\1\ 6\ 5\ 6\ 6\end{array}$$

The next step is to deal with the new line of figures in just the same way and thus obtain a third line:

$$\begin{array}{c}5\ 5\ 1\ 4\ 2\ 4\\1\ 6\ 5\ 6\ 6\\7\ 2\ 2\ 3\end{array}$$

NAMES AND NUMBERS 41

and so continue until the whole pyramid is completed, thus:

$$5\ 5\ 1\ 4\ 2\ 4$$
$$1\ 6\ 5\ 6\ 6$$
$$7\ 2\ 2\ 3$$
$$9\ 4\ 5$$
$$4\ 9$$
$$4$$

This gives the figure 4 as the result of the inquiry, and as this is a negative Sun-number we have to reply in the negative, or perhaps add that if you get your wish it will not be worth having. The Sun, of course, is always there, but its power in the winter is nothing like what it is in the summer, and Nature responds accordingly.

But this example is only to show the manner of working, and I need hardly say that a question which always got the same answer need never be asked. How, then, are we to proceed in regular practice of this ancient method of divination by numbers? In a word we have to take out the values of the letters under the Sun or Moon lines of action, as given in the beginning of this chapter, add the values for each word together, reduce them to unit value, and set that figure down in place of the word. Then the procedure is the same as we have shown above.

Only you must be careful to note that in the morning and evening you use the Sun line of letter-values, and in the afternoon and night you use the Moon line.

I have now said enough about this old system of divination to get you busy for quite a long time; and whether in the day time or the night to gain the advantage of your own ingenuity and labour.

In translating the values derived from the Pyramid, the final number being—

1. It promises success whether by one's own efforts or by the help and patronage of men of position and power.

2. It produces failure through vacillation and uncertainty. It denotes lack of will-power and the unfortunate influence of women.

3. This gives success and gain, with increase and expansion. Great hopes realised. Good efforts rewarded.

4. This denotes failure of projects or at most but indifferent success, many rivalries and affronts.

5. Gain through the use of the faculties, success through correspondence or travelling. Knowledge is power.

6. Favours and benefits from young women, and a happy result to all efforts. Success with pleasure and contentment.

7. Success through the good offices of matrons or married women of position and influence. Travelling and commerce with the people. Public honours.

8. Failure through jealousy, mistrust, or lack of effort. Loss and possibly privation. Many obstacles and hindrances.

9. Success through effort and enterprise. There will be rivalries and contests, but you will gain your object by force of your own will-power.

If you will refer to the descriptions of the planets given in Chapter I, you will be able to frame your own answer from the index number at the head of the pyramid. In my illustration the pyramid is reversed, as it was found easier to handle that way in print; but any builder will tell you that the proper way is to lay down the base line first of all, and then each successive course on top until you come to the apex or pinnacle, and this represents the headstone or capital from which you may look afar and see the end from the beginning.

Chapter V

THE MAGIC SQUARE

This is a very ancient form of divination by numbers, which is to be found among the oldest Chinese records, and is commonly known to us as the "Fifteen Puzzle." It consists of a square of figures from 1 to 9, so arranged that whichever way you add them up, whether from the top to bottom, or across or diagonally, they always amount to 15. The ancients put them in this order:

```
    4   9   2

    3   5   7

    8   1   6
```

This gives the following resolutions:

492 equals 15
357 ,, 15
816 ,, 15
258 ,, 15
654 ,, 15
438 ,, 15
159 ,, 15
672 ,, 15

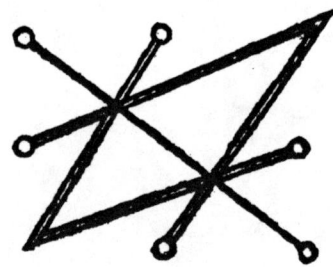

THE MAGIC SQUARE 45

and the sum of all the figures is of course 45, which is three times 15. In order to preserve this form they joined up the figures 1, 2, 3 by a line, then 4, 5, 6, by another line and lastly 7, 8, 9 by a third line similar to the first, and thus produced this glyph or form as a mnemonic or memoriser.

They said that the figure 5 in the centre represented Man as the conscious principle or knower of things, and the eight numbers surrounding it they called the "eightfold path" or Pa-tao. But modernly we have made another use of it by resetting the figures according to the new development of thought and activity in the world, and we divide them into three groups:

> The Sun 1, Mars 9, and Jupiter 3, are spiritual numbers.
> Venus 6, Mercury 5, and the Moon 7, are mental numbers.
> The Sun 4, Saturn 8, and Moon 2 are physical.

This is the result of experiment guided by astrological knowledge.

We then have this arrangement:

3	1	9
6	7	5
2	8	4

46 FORTUNE TELLING BY NUMBERS

This Table is applied to the date of a person's birth. Thus if one should be born on March 13, 1889, we have the figures 13/3/89, the centuries being omitted as common to all, and we find these numbers, and place them in a new chart, thus:

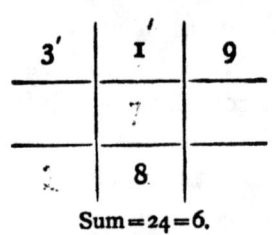

3'	1'	9
	7	
	8	

Sum = 24 = 6.

It will be noticed that the repetition of the figure 3 in the date is shown by a tick or accent and it strengthens the significance of that number in the life.

The sum of all the figures in the date is 24, and their unit value is 6, which is Venus.

When two planetary numbers occupy adjacent squares they are said to be in conjunction, but when a square divides them they are in opposition. Thus in the above figure we have—

> Conjunction of Jupiter 3 and Sun 1,
> Conjunction of Sun 1 and Mars 9,
> Opposition of Sun 1 and Saturn 8.

This indicates great success, gain and increase of position and influence, strong executive powers, conquests, aspirations, zeal and industry; but also

THE MAGIC SQUARE

some serious impediments, obstacles and hindrances. Generally, a strong inspirational nature, tending to symmetry and harmonious expression. The keynote, being that of 6 Venus, gives this latter interpretation. With 9 Mars as the sum of the figures we should have a far more forceful and even a militant person inspired by high endeavours.

Looking at this date astrologically we find on the date 13/3/89 Moon conjunction Saturn, impediments, obstacles; Mercury sextile Mars, zeal, enterprise, endeavour; Mercury trine Uranus, ingenuity and constructional faculty, a synthetic mind; Venus strong in its own sign Taurus in trine aspect to Jupiter. These indications agree very well indeed with those derived from the Number.

In taking any date it should be observed that for this purpose the day begins at noon and ends on the following noon. Thus the 19th of the month at 3 a.m. is really the 18th at 15 hours after noon. So that any person born between midnight and noon, that is, within six hours before or after sunrise, must be taken as born on the preceding date.

Before we go further it will be well to state the general natures and significations of the planets, as by their numbers:

(1.) Positive Sun—Glory, fame, achievement, success, honours, influence and rulership or control according to the measure of the individual powers. Good health, long life.

2. Negative Moon—Changes, mutations, public disorders, infections, suasions. Evil influence of women. Weakness of will, indecision, inconstancy. Unfortunate journeys. Decrease, loss, ineptitude. Ineffectual effort, failure.

3. Jupiter—Increase, expansion, hopefulness, confidence, buoyancy, aptitude, generosity or extravagance, nobility or pomposity according to the degree of intelligence enjoyed. Riches, productiveness, fulness, and success.

4. The Sun negative—Partial success only, lack of influence and power of direction, desire for position unsatisfied, or position gained by loss of dignity and independence, vanity, false pride, a master only among small people, successful on the other side of the equator.

5. Mercury—Intellect, desire for knowledge, aptitude, a good memory, well informed, sometimes a busybody and chatterer, but always a great talker and very attentive to detail. Good commercial instincts, clever manipulator, a messenger, carrier, correspondent, often a traveller or linguist, a man of letters or a scientist.

6. Venus—A sympathetic and well-disposed nature, fond of music, singing, dancing and rhythm. Endowed with artistic faculty and generally possessed of a fine sense of pose and symmetry. The social and domestic virtues (and their complement of vices) are represented here, and the mental faculties tend

THE MAGIC SQUARE

to the fine arts, music, poetry, painting, drawing, etc. Success through social and artistic pursuits.

7. The Moon positive—Travelling, publicity, management of peoples, public works, controller of public supplies, caterers, etc. The fortunes lie in the direction of public representation and the pursuit of popular projects and aims. Sometimes by catering to public needs and the supply of amusements. A strong, forceful and magnetic personality. Successful.

8. Saturn—Obstacles, hindrances, privations, loss, hurt, defects, impediments. Either deeply philosophical and out of touch with the world, or sordid and out of sympathy with it. In most cases misanthropic.

9. Mars—Energetic, enterprising, executive, strong, virile, and forceful. Freedom, zeal, keenness, and love of liberty. It shows courage and enterprise and desire for pioneer work and the conquering of new worlds. It gives enthusiasm and ambition and disposes to fevers. But it may produce a firebrand and strong partisan, with more zeal than discretion and a disposition to lawlessness, or freedom in disregard of law. Thus the man is either pioneer or pirate. But always capable of self-assertion.

o—Universality, vacuity, space, a cosmopolitan spirit, astronomer, navigator, discoverer. Sometimes the index of insanity. Either very wide sympathies or entire lack of self-control and stability. This figure must always be read in connection with the

50 FORTUNE TELLING BY NUMBERS

sum of the chart when it occurs in the date of birth.

Let us take a few instances as examples of the working of this Magic Square of Fortune. When dates are taken from the Old Style calendar they must be reduced to their modern equivalents. Thus:

Oliver Cromwell born O.S. April 25, 1599, which is the same as May 4 in the New Style calendar. The sun on both dates will then be the same in longitude. We, therefore, take out the figure—

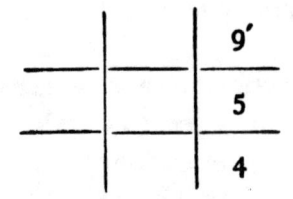

		9′
		5
		4

Sum = 27 or 9.
Conjunction of Mars and Sun.
Conjunction of Sun and Mercury.

He was a great zealot and a great patriot, a born soldier, most highly efficient and executive, and a man of considerable acumen, both destructive and constructive, a man of decision and action.

His secretary was the poet, John Milton, who was born on December 19, 1608 (New Style). This gives the figures 19/12/08. The chart is as follows:

THE MAGIC SQUARE

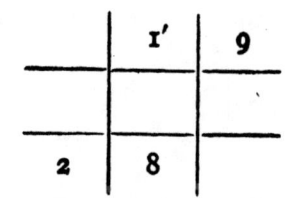

	1′	9
2	8	

Sum 21 or 3 Jupiter.
Conjunction—Sun and Mars.
Conjunction—Moon and Saturn.
Opposition—Sun and Saturn.

The poet is here defined as a subject of Jupiter, which very well accords with his nature and work. But we see there are some impediments not only to his spiritual aspirations as by Saturn opposing the Sun, but also physically by the conjunction of the Moon and Saturn. The 0 occurring in the date of birth gives the cosmopolitan touch to the character. He travelled extensively in France and Italy. He was elevated by his talent to a high position, as denoted by the double Sun, was associated with the martial efforts of Cromwell (Mars conjunct Sun), and after three years went blind through overwork (Moon conjunct Saturn).

The horoscope of Milton shows Sagittarius rising, so that he was rightly a subject of Jupiter, as shown above.

Napoleon I., from August 14, 1769, shows 14869 or 28/1 as the sum of the Chart, with conjunctions of Sun and Mars, Sun (negative) and Saturn, and an opposi-

52 FORTUNE TELLING BY NUMBERS

tion of Saturn to Sun. Here is the Chart, of which the sum is 1 (positive Sun).

	1	9
6		
	8	4

It shows as clearly as possible the military ambitions and conquests of the great Dictator, with his subsequent fall, exile, and wasting disease.

The Chart of Horatio Nelson, 23/5/19, shows a double Mars in conjunction with Mercury and a negative Moon in conjunction with Saturn. The latter position clearly indicates the physical deprivation which he suffered in the loss of arm and eye. The double Mars gave him his redoubtable fighting powers, and its conjunction with Mercury shows the agility, alertness, and resourcefulness of his brain.

King Louis XVI. of France, 23/8/54, has the following remarkable chart:

3		
		5
2	8	4

The Sun is a negative Sun or 4. But look at the physical base on which his destiny was upheld. It contains Saturn in conjunction with both the Sun and

Moon. The only other conjunction was that of Sun and Mercury, rendered weak and impotent by its negative associations. For what could Mercury gain from a negative Sun already vitiated by its conjunctions with Saturn? In effect the monarch was deposed and executed, and his son consigned to prison, where he died.

We thus see how remarkable the birth-date falls into line with the facts when viewed from the point of Numbers and their associated planetary indications.

Chapter VI

PHONETIC VALUES

Although we have clearly shown that there is a definite value attaching to certain letters when applied to a particular purpose by specific rules of procedure, it may be of more than passing interest to my readers to know that there are other means employed and other matters involved than mere character reading and fortune telling by numbers.

The Kabalists have a traditional sound-value attached to every letter of the alphabet in its various inflexions by means of which the sum of a name can be directly related to any period of time, and the chances of its recognition and success at that time may be certainly known.

Take, for instance, the common experience of winning numbers in lotteries. One would not think that there are any laws governing these apparently chance results, or the name of any race-horse which wins at a given time on any date. If you imagine for a moment that these things are the result of mere chance as distinguished from law, I can tell you at once that you are entirely wrong. Nothing happens

PHONETIC VALUES

by chance in a universe that is governed by law. You may cover up your ignorance of that law by a label with a name on it, but that will not prevent the law from determining the event just as it is bound to happen, nor prevent those who understand the law from predicting the nature of the event.

Let me give some few instances of this fact. But first we must know the traditional sound-values of the letters of the alphabet.

1. Letters A as in "father"; long I, as in "mice"; E, and double E.
2. B; short U, as in "must"; R, K, hard G, as in "go"; short O, as in "not"; double P.
3. J; soft G, as in "gentle"; Ch, as in "church"; L.
4. D, T, M.
5. H, N.
6. Long U, as in "flute"; OO as in "root"; V. W, S,
7. Z, and final S, as in "blazes"; U, as in "mute."
8. P, F.
9. Double T, as in "matter."

Note: Short I, as in "kit," is never represented.

Now let us look at some of the results that are derived from racing, where the names of the horses are the basis of the calculation, and the planetary day and hour the determining factors of success. It

56 FORTUNE TELLING BY NUMBERS

should be noted that only those letters which contribute to the sound of the name are of value.

On Wednesday (Mercury) 5 and in the hour of the same planet 5, value 10 or 1:

    Silvester—6361642—28—1 won at 5 to 1 against.

On the same day and in the hour of the Moon—57—3:

    Pastures New—816327 516—39—3 won at 10 to 1.

On Tuesday in the hour of Mars—9:

    Genevieve—3151616—23—5 (negative to 9) won.
    Ardvreck—1246212—18—9 won.

On Saturday in the hour of Jupiter—2:

    Stonyford—646518224—38—2 won.

On Thursday in the hour of the Sun—31—4:

    Amphitryon—1484225—26—8 (negative of 4) won.

On Thursday in the hour of Saturn—38—2:

    King Sol—252 623—2 won.

On Wednesday in the hour of Moon—57—12—3:

    Furore—87222—21—3 won.

These examples will serve to show that there is a veritable law of sound-values—in other words, vibrations—which answers to the facts as we know them.

Hundreds of instances might have been given to show that this law of vibratory sequence is not only directly linked up with planetary sequence—the order of the planets being always that of their relative apparent motions—but that the sequence is equally expressed in tone, colour, and number.

But if this be thought too great a claim on the uninformed credulity of the average reader, I fear that my claim to be able to indicate the weight carried by a winning horse, in seven cases out of every sequential ten, will have small chance of credence. Nevertheless it is a fact, and those who have subscribed to my private issue of " The Eclipse System " know that it is so, to their great advantage. Thus it indicated Furore to win the Cesarewitch, and it did so at 100 to 7 against. It also showed Brown Prince or Planet (both carrying the same weight) to win the Cambridgeshire Stakes. Brown Prince won at 100 to 6, and Planet was 2nd at 100 to 7.

Then again it showed Planet to win the November Handicap at Manchester, and it did so at 10 to 1 against, with many consecutive events in between these popular contests, some of which I have used here to show that sound-values are a useful guide to successful speculation when scientifically used. That they have failed in other hands was due to the fact that the underlying planetary causes were unknown, and many fictitious factors were brought into use.

58 FORTUNE TELLING BY NUMBERS

I may now indicate the winning or lucky numbers in every day and hour, from sunrise to sunset:

Sunday—Hour of Sun	... Lucky Number	2
,,	Venus	,, ,,	7
,,	Mercury	,, ,,	6
,,	Moon	,, ,,	8
,,	Saturn	,, ,,	9
,,	Jupiter	,, ,,	4
,,	Mars	,, ,,	1
Monday ,,	Moon	,, ,,	5
,,	Saturn	,, ,,	6
,,	Jupiter	,, ,,	1
,,	Mars	,, ,,	7
,,	Sun	,, ,,	8
,,	Venus	,, ,,	4
,,	Mercury	,, ,,	3
Tuesday ,,	Mars	,, ,,	9
,,	Sun	,, ,,	1
,,	Venus	,, ,,	6
,,	Mercury	,, ,,	5
,,	Moon	,, ,,	7
,,	Saturn	,, ,,	8
,,	Jupiter	,, ,,	3
Wednesday ,,	Mercury	,, ,,	1
,,	Moon	,, ,,	3
,,	Saturn	,, ,,	4
,,	Jupiter	,, ,,	8
,,	Mars	,, ,,	5

PHONETIC VALUES 59

	Hour of Sun	... Lucky Number	6
	,, Venus ...	,, ,,	2
Thursday	,, Jupiter ...	,, ,,	6
	,, Mars ...	,, ,,	3
	,, Sun ...	,, ,,	4
	,, Venus ...	,, ,,	9
	,, Mercury ...	,, ,,	8
	,, Moon ...	,, ,,	1
	,, Saturn ...	,, ,,	2
Friday	,, Venus ...	,, ,,	3
	,, Mercury ...	,, ,,	2
	,, Moon ...	,, ,,	4
	,, Saturn ...	,, ,,	5
	,, Jupiter ...	,, ,,	9
	,, Mars ...	,, ,,	6
	,, Sun ...	,, ,,	7
Saturday	,, Saturn ...	,, ,,	7
	,, Jupiter ...	,, ,,	2
	,, Mars ...	,, ,,	8
	,, Sun ...	,, ,,	9
	,, Venus ...	,, ,,	5
	,, Mercury ...	,, ,,	4
	,, Moon ...	,, ,,	6

These numbers will prove fortunate to those whose names, when calculated according to the Sun and Moon Table of Values, are of the same value as the Lucky Number. The strongest combination is that which arises from the admixture of two planets which are friendly to one another, as—

>Mars and the Sun,
>Moon and Venus,
>Moon and Jupiter,
>Venus and Jupiter,
>Mercury and Saturn.

But to be fortunate to an individual that person's name-value must be in vibratory sympathy with the Lucky Number of the Hour, for it is the combined values of the day and hour planets, and nothing can withstand it while its hour shall last.

Those who believe in "luck" will do well in the light of these pages to reform their notions and change their labels so as to include the established fact of numerical sequence and the law of periodicity in a universe that is all life and vibration, where nothing of chance can set its foot, and where "luck" is only another name for personal resonance or response to the ceaseless interplay of cosmic forces.

Those who have patiently studied the various aspects of this great law of Numerical Sequence in daily life will improve their knowledge immensely by the study of my "Arcana," which finds its public only by personal request and by private circulation under a binding agreement.

To the general reader of these pages who may only seek amusement and recreation, a most fascinating and delightful study has now been opened up, by which, with a little patience and practice, very remarkable and satisfactory readings may be made for one's friends. And **since** knowledge is power, let us see that it be harmless and benevolent, and even useful. **For the virtue of everything is in its use.**

PREFACE

It is usual for a preface to be apologetic. This one is only half an apology. There are many dream-books of all sorts and sizes; ponderous tomes on the one hand, penny shockers on the other. This is a compromise. The writer is convinced that there is much more in dreaming than some of the scientists allow. On the other hand, there is, perhaps, less in interpretation than some fanatics would have us to believe. Midway, possibly, is that haven of desire, the happy medium. The writer has done his best to balance the scale. It is hoped that this work will inform a few and interest, if not instruct, many more.

J. W.

DREAMS AND VISIONS
SOME WONDERFUL EXAMPLES

LEST it be thought that dreams are only idle fancies which deserve neither attention nor explanation, it will be as well to say at once that for many years past a large body of well-educated persons and men of science have devoted much time to the question of what dreams are and how they are caused. The scientists are those who study mental or mind processes, and their science is psychology.

The other persons referred to are engaged in psychic research, investigating unusual happenings that are well vouched for. Both psychologists and psychic researchers have a large body of evidence to work upon, and the results of their studies and their explanations fill many big books.

There are very few of us who do not dream. And sometimes these dreams are of so vivid a nature that they make a great impression at the time, and linger long in the memory. So real are many of these dreams that it would seem impossible for us to believe that we are not actually living through the experiences we have at the time.

This makes us think that the dreaming state may have its laws: that it may be a condition of existence governed by special arrangements, of a different character certainly, but otherwise not unlike our earth life. With this statement generally many psychologists would agree. Other dreams we have at times that are just confused jumbles of thoughts and sights and sounds. These may well have a direct physical cause, and we need not bother with them at all.

It is with the real dreams that we are concerned here; with the dreams that are more or less orderly and sequential; with dreams that may be strange, but are more or less clear and well developed.

And here we must distinguish between two great classes of these dreams—ordinary dreams, of action or suffering, and visions. The latter are sometimes very vivid. They are generally of the nature of things or persons seen; as though the dreamer were an observer merely, instead of being concerned directly with the dream, and an actor in the drama that is being unfolded.

Little need be said of the antiquity of dreams. From time immemorial there have been dreams and dreamers. Even the brutes dream sometimes. Who has not seen a dog whine and whimper uneasily in his sleep as it sees and hears things?

Perhaps the earliest dreams to be recorded are those in the Bible: of King Abimelech warned against taking Abram's wife (whom the patriarch had falsely called his sister); the

DREAMS AND VISIONS

dreams and visions of Jacob and Laban; of Joseph, of Solomon, of Daniel. All these readily recur to the mind.

Nearer to us in point of time are the visions which have appeared to the saints, to Joan of Arc, to the Maid of Lourdes, and to many others all through the ages.

There is little need, however, to demonstrate the point that dreams and visions occur. We all of us experience them. What we are more anxious to know is, What do they portend? Are they of the nature of warnings of what is to happen? Is there any one method of interpreting them?

To these questions, too, there is a very good reply provided in many books on the subject. Numberless instances are given, on the best and most credible authority, of warnings received in dreams. Some of these will be referred to later. Other dreams have been of places and persons never previously seen, but which were recognised afterwards as having been actually seen in the dreams.

Some wonderful examples of dreams are given in a book called "The Other World," by the Rev. F. G. Lee. One or two of these are worth reference. They are all vouched for, and given in full in the very words of the dreamer in the book.

A gentleman in Cornwall dreamed that he witnessed a murder of the Chancellor of the Exchequer in the House of Commons. He had never been there in his life. He told several people of this dream, and described the dress and the position in the lobby of the murderer and his victim. Next day—this happened a hundred years ago—a rider with news came into the village and confirmed the circumstances of the tragedy.

Soon afterwards the gentleman went to London, and in the lobby pointed out where he had seen in his dream the Chancellor and his assailant stand. Those who were present testified that it had happened just as he said.

Another wonderful dream was that which occurred to the mother of Maria Marten. Her daughter had been taken away from her home and betrayed, under promise of marriage, and then murdered. Time passed, and the supposed husband of Maria wrote to say that they were married and living abroad. But the mother dreamed that her daughter had been murdered and her body buried in a barn.

So strong was her impression that when search was made the body was found and showed traces of foul play. Corder, the seducer and murderer, was found, confessed to his crime after trial, and was executed in 1828.

Not less remarkable was that of the rector of a parish, one of whose congregation had recently died. The deceased was a wealthy man who was believed to have left no will. Great injustice would have been done by this, as the estates passed to a distant branch of the family, leaving others in dire straits.

The rector dreamed on three occasions that the deceased appeared to him and indicated that a will had been made. Each time further details

DREAMS AND VISIONS

were given. On the last occasion the rector dreamed that he went to London, to Staple Inn (he had never been there), to a certain house, and to a certain room. A picture of Lord Eldon was hung in the room, and details, such as a particular drawer in which the will would be found, were given.

So vivid was the dream that the rector told it to a clerical friend, who accompanied him to London. They found the house, the offices, the room, the drawer—and there was the will.

In each of these cases it will be remarked that there has been a dead person concerned in giving a message to a living one. This seems strongly to confirm the view that the mind or soul is still active when the body is dead. In other words, it points to the fact of the survival of the soul.

It also shows that the inner mind is most active. It can receive a message best when the body is at rest. But the living can also, when in great distress, send a message to a dreamer.

A native in the Channel Islands dreamed very vividly that persons in great danger were calling him from the rocks. He fell asleep again, and the dream was repeated more violently. Next morning early he went down to the quay and told his mates. They were not inclined to believe him. But as he persisted they launched a boat and pulled off to some rocks far away. There they found several persons nearly dead with hunger, cold, and exposure. A lighthouse was afterwards built there.

Instances of this kind could be multiplied a

hundredfold to show how dreams have been fulfilled after the warning has been received. But there is another kind of dream that we now have to consider—that in which the dreamer does not so much receive a message as see or hear something that is going to happen.

The "message dreams" are to be explained scientifically by telepathy. Another little book in this series will deal with this fully. Telepathy means the communication of two minds, without the ordinary means of conveying a message at a distance.

In many cases the one who sends the message does not know that he has sent it. The need is very urgent. The mind is in great distress or danger, and the message goes out. The person who receives it is in the best condition to get it only when the body is passive—in sleep, for example—and the mind more than usually receptive of impressions of this nature.

But the other dreams, in which a knowledge, often more or less dim and confused, is obtained of what is going to happen, are explainable in a different way. It was said before that the inner mind possesses extraordinary powers. It is not hampered with the conceptions of time and space. Australia is as near, in thought, as the picture hanging on the wall. Next month, or next year, or even later, is only the extension of the present, seen as the present.

In dreams the inner mind exercises these great powers of clairvoyance and clairaudience —it sees and hears the future as the present; it sees and hears what is happening in the distance as though it were itself there. The mind, in dreaming, is believed to have a mind-body, which it uses outside the limits of time and space.

Now, so long as these dreams are intelligible, they may be trusted to tell their own story. The difficulty arises when the dream is more or less of a parable. There is, then, the necessity for an interpretation.

Few of us forget the dream of Pharaoh and the wonderful interpretation given by Joseph, who was promoted to be the ruler of the whole land of Egypt, second only to the King. The dream of Pharaoh was a parable, and needed to be interpreted. Joseph had earned his reputation as a translator of dreams before that time. The captain of the guard had dreamed, and it was Joseph who explained it, and it came to pass.

Joseph also, as we know from the tale of his brethren when sent back to their father with the corn and the money and Joseph's cup in Benjamin's sack, was a diviner. Joseph's servant charged the children of Israel with stealing the cup in which "my lord divineth." Joseph used divination to foretell the future.

Around the subject of dreams there has arisen a lore of interpretation. If one dreams of certain things, this means that something of a particular kind will happen. No one knows exactly how this came about. For many generations—for hundreds and thousands of years—there have been interpreters of dreams, and gradually some of this interpretation has been collected and written down. Some of it does not agree with other statements.

But no doubt, like most other things which have grown in the same way—the knowledge of herbs and poisons, of the stars and star-lore, of palmistry and the other occult, or secret, arts—there is some truth in all of them, even if it be hidden at the bottom of a well, and is sometimes a little difficult to get at.

A great scientific work, dealing with psychology—the study of the mind processes—called "Fact and Fable in Psychology," by Professor Jastrow, and published a few years ago, gives the following as current beliefs which have perhaps arisen by the growth of analogy, or correspondence in similarity between the dream and its reputed meaning.

To dream of using glue, for example, means imprisonment for yourself or for your friend. To dream of pineapples betokens crosses and troubles. To dream of going up a ladder means good fortune; of coming down, one of poverty and misfortune to come. To dream of dirt or mud foretells that you will be abused and slandered. To dream of being on stilts indicates that one is unduly puffed up and proud. To dream of gathering fruit from an old tree means that one will succeed to the wealth of some ancient person.

If you dream of a clock, and the hands stop, it means death; but if the hands keep moving, it means recovery from sickness. To dream of a concert means harmony with those we love. To dream of earthworms means that we have secret enemies trying to ruin us.

DREAMS AND VISIONS

To dream of onions or garlic or leek means the betrayal of secrets. To wash the hands means relief from anxieties. To have one's foot cut off means that a proposed journey will be prevented.

He who dreams he has lost a tooth will lose a friend. He who dreams that a rib is taken out of his side will ere long see the death of his wife. To dream of swimming and wading is good so long as the head be kept above water.

Some dreams depend upon contrast, and not similarity, for their interpretation. To be married denotes that some of one's kinsfolk are dead. To dream of death denotes happiness and long life. Hence has arisen the saying that " dreams go by the contrary."

Then again there are modes of interpretation by which the significance of a dream is reversed by virtue of the sex of the dreamer. The Zulus and the Maoris cling closely to the interpretation of dreams by contraries. To dream that a sick friend is dead is a sign that he will recover. To dream of a wedding is to hear of a death.

But many other dreams are not so simple. They are so mixed up with other things, and seem to come in such a way that it is not easy to see what they mean. It is here that a book like this one is helpful. It aids the dreamer to find out what the dream may mean. Then, again, we often find that we remember only a part of the dream. But if we think of that, and try to find out what it means, it often helps us to recover the other parts.

There have always been dreamers. And

there have always been those who could explain the dreams. Back in the dim past, in the early ages of the world, wise men dwelt upon the subject, and the result of their learning was handed down. Certain dreams were found to be followed by certain events. It was then thought that the dream of a particular object meant that the dreamer would have some particular experience. This fixed the meaning of dreams.

And when it was found to be right in many instances, these explanations or interpretations of dreams became valuable and were usefully preserved. Many of the interpretations which are given in this book have been handed down from the time of the Greeks and the Assyrians, who lived thousands of years ago. They were noted for their great wisdom on these matters.

In sleep, as has been suggested earlier, the mind is much more free than when we are awake. It is able during sleep to roam freely through time and space. This is why the future is often foretold in dreams. It sometimes happens, too, that we are able to solve an old difficulty regarding that which had occurred long before.

In dreams the mind sees everything as the present: there is neither past nor future in dreaming. So, also, with regard to distance. In dreams we may visit the other side of the world in a moment and return as quickly.

Often in dreams we see things and persons and places that in reality we are only destined to see at some future time. Often, too, we find when we see a place for the first time in our waking life that it seems so familiar that we have visited it before. We have really seen it in our dreams, and then perhaps have forgotten all about it till we see it in reality.

That dream, perhaps, was given to us for a purpose. And if we had made a habit of remembering our dreams and thinking over them we should be helped and guided much more than we are. For it is in sleep that we receive guidance.

The old Scripture passage which says, "He giveth to His beloved sleep," when properly translated, reads, "He giveth to His beloved *in* sleep"—a very different thing. In the old times men were warned in a dream to do this and not to do that. To-day it is the same. We have dreams, and many of them are warnings.

That there is need for interpretations of dreams is seen when we remember that Pharaoh of old had to call to his aid Joseph to explain his dreams of the ears of corn and of the lean and fat kine. There are other examples of dreams that require explaining that will be remembered by most persons.

On the other hand, there are many wonderful dreams that have been fulfilled to the very letter. Particulars of these have been recorded. But nearly all of us know some friend who has had a dream every part of which happened just as it was seen in the vision.

But these straightforward dreams are the exception. They do not often happen so. Generally our dreams are of different things, and are not very plain to us.

It is because of this that the dream-book is helpful. It helps in two ways. It gives an idea, or suggestion, as to what the dream may portend, what its warning is ; and it also helps, by fixing the mind upon the dream itself, to bring back other parts of the dream.

In using the book, then, as much of the dream as possible should be recalled, and all the indications looked up.

The various explanations for the different parts should then be put together, and this be taken as a whole, to suggest the meaning of the dream. This may not seem to be easy ; but it will be found with a little practice that much help will be derived from the study of dreams.

In the next section of this book we give a selection of interpretations that have come down to us from early Roman times. Many of these interpretations are the work of Artemidorus, who flourished in the reign of Antoninus and wrote a learned book on dreams. An edition of this book—perhaps the best—was published in Paris in 1604, and was translated by Rigaltius.

ANCIENT INTERPRETATIONS
TRANSLATED FROM ARTEMIDORUS

Acquaintance.—To dream that you fight with them signifies distraction, especially if the person so dreaming be sick.

Adversary.—To dream that you receive obstructions from him, shows that you shall despatch your business speedily.

Air.—To dream that you see it clear and serene denotes the discovery of lost goods, or things that have been stolen. If the person so dreaming be at law, it shows he shall overthrow his adversary; and if he designs a voyage or journey, it shows he shall be successful therein. And, in short, all good things are denoted by a clear and serene air. But to dream the air is cloudy, dark, and troubled, denotes to the dreamer sadness, grief, sickness, melancholy, loss of goods, hindrance of business, and is in all things the reverse of dreaming what we have before mentioned of a clear and serene air.

Almonds.—To dream one sees or eats almonds signifies difficulty and trouble.

Alms.—To dream they are begged of you, and you deny to give them, shows want and misery to the dreamer; but to dream that you give them freely is a sign of great joy and long life to the dreamer or some particular friend.

Altar.—To dream that you discover or uncover an altar betokens joy and gladness.

Angel.—To dream you see an angel or angels is very good, and to dream that you yourself are one is much better. But to speak with or call upon them is of evil signification. And to dream that you see an angel fly over you or your house signifies joy, consolation, benediction, and good news, and shows increase of honour and authority.

Angling.—To dream you are angling betokens much affliction and trouble in seeking for something you desire to get.

Bagpipes.—To dream that you play upon bagpipes signifies trouble, contention, and being overthrown at law.

Barley-bread.—To dream of eating barley-bread signifies health and content.

Bees.—To dream of bees is good and bad; good, if they sting not; but bad, if they sting the party dreaming, for then they signify enemies.

Bells.—To dream that one hears ringing of bells, if of a sanguine complexion, brings him good news; but to others it shows alarms, murmurings, disturbances, and commotions among citizens.

Bleeding.—To dream of bleeding at the nose signifies loss of goods and decay of riches to those who are phlegmatic and melancholy; but to the choleric and sanguine it signifies health and joy.

ANCIENT INTERPRETATIONS

Boots.—To dream that one is well booted or hath good boots on signifies honour and profit by servants.

Buried.—For a man to dream that he is buried and interred signifies he shall have as much wealth as he hath earth laid over him.

Cards.—To dream one plays at cards or dice signifies deceit and craft, and that he is in danger of losing his estate by some wicked person. And yet playing at cards, tables, or any game in a dream shows the party shall be very fortunate if the tables allude to love.

Cat.—If anyone dreams that he hath encountered a cat or killed one, he will commit a thief to prison and prosecute him to the death, for the cat signifies a common thief. If he dreams that he eats cat's flesh, he will have the goods of the thief that robbed him; if he dream he hath the skin, then he will have all the thief's goods. If anyone dreams he fought with a cat that scratched him sorely, that denotes some sickness or affliction.

Caterpillars.—To dream you see caterpillars signifies ill-luck and misfortune from secret enemies.

Cheese.—To dream you eat cheese signifies profit and gain.

Chickens.—To dream of a hen and her chickens signifies loss and damage.

Command.—To dream you command one signifies trouble; to dream you see one command signifies anger and authority.

Confections.—To dream that one makes confections and sweetmeats betokens pleasure and profit.

Corns.—For a man to dream that his flesh is full of corns shows he will grow rich proportionately to the corns.

Crown.—To dream of having a crown of gold on your head signifies the friendship of your liege; and the dreamer will be honoured by many persons and will have many gifts.

Dead Folks.—To dream of talking with dead folks is a good, auspicious dream, and signifies a boldness of courage and a very clear conscience.

Devil.—If any dream that he sees the devil, it is a very bad sign, for such a vision cannot bring along with it any good tidings. To the sick it foretells death; and to the healthful it signifies melancholy, anger, tumults, and violent sickness. If any dream the devil speaks to him, it signifies temptation, deceit, treachery, despair, and sometimes the ruin and death of him that dreams.

Drink.—To drink warm water is bad; to drink muddy water is very bad; to drink clear water is a good sign; to drink thick wine is very good; to drink white wine signifies health; to drink milk is an exceedingly good sign; to drink vinegar signifies discomfort.

Eagle.—To dream that an eagle is seen in some high place is a good sign to those that undertake some weighty business, and especially to soldiers. If one dream that an eagle lights upon his head, it signifies death to the dreamer; and the same if he dreams that he is carried into the air by an eagle. An eagle flying strongly, and falling upon the head of him that dreameth, certainly signifies his death. To be mounted on an eagle signifies to kings, princes, and mighty and rich personages, death; but to the poor it is good, for they shall be welcome and received of all rich men, from whom they shall receive great profit. Oftentimes it causeth changing one's country and going to another nation. The eagle threatening signifieth the threatening of some great personage. But to dream of his being gentle or giving anything, or to dream that he spake, hath been found a good dream by experience. To see an eagle that is dead is good for a servant and him that is in fear, for it denotes the death of the master and threatener; and unto others shows that a stop shall be put to their affairs, for a dead eagle can do nothing.

Eat.—To dream of eating human flesh signifies labour and distress; to eat lard or salt signifies murmuring; to eat cheese signifies gain and profit; to eat apples signifies anger.

Eggs.—To dream of eggs signifies gain and profit, especially to physicians, painters, and to those who sell and trade with them. To dream you see broken eggs is a very ill sign, and signifies loss to the party dreaming.

Face.—To dream you see a fresh, taking, smiling face and countenance is a sign of friendship and joy. To dream you see a meagre, pale face is a sign of trouble, poverty, and death. To dream one washes his face denotes repentance of sin. A black face signifies long life.

Fields.—To dream of fields and pleasant places shows to a man that he will marry a discreet, chaste, and beautiful wife, and that she will bear him very handsome children. And to a woman it betokens a loving and prudent husband, by whom she shall have beautiful children.

Figs.—To dream you see figs in season is a good dream, and signifies joy and pleasure; but out of season, the contrary.

Fruit.—To dream of fruit has a different interpretation, according to what the fruit is. Apples show long life and success; a boy to a woman with child; cheerfulness in your sweetheart, and riches in trade. Cherries indicate disappointment in love and vexation in the married state.

Frogs.—To dream of frogs is good for them that live upon the commons. But as to frogs in general, they signifiy flatterers, indifferent and different babblers, abusers, and praters.

Geese.—To dream you hear the cackling of geese signifies profit, assurance, and despatch of business.

Gloves.—To dream one has gloves on his hands signifies honour and safety.

Gold.—To dream your clothes are embroidered with gold signifies joy and honour. If a man dreams that he gathers up gold and

ANCIENT INTERPRETATIONS

silver, that signifies deceit and loss. If anyone dreams that his pockets are full of gold, it betokeneth that he shall receive but little money. To dream one hath a crown of gold upon his head signifies favour with his sovereign and that he shall be honoured and feared by many. For a man to dream that he hath found gold, and cannot tell where to hide it, or that he is afraid to be taken with it, shows he shall have a wife who shall rob his purse and take away all his money while he is asleep.

Grapes.—To dream of eating grapes at any time signifies cheerfulness and profit. To tread grapes signifies the overthrow of enemies. To gather white grapes signifies gain, but to dream of gathering black grapes signifies damage.

Hail.—To dream of hail signifies sorrow and trouble, and sometimes that the most hidden secrets shall be revealed and made known.

Hat.—To dream that your hat is broken or fallen off means damage and dishonour.

Hell.—To dream of descending into hell, and returning thence to those who are rich signifies misfortune, but it is a good sign to the poor and weak.

Hunger.—To dream one is extraordinarily hungry and that his appetite craves sustenance, shows that he will be ingenious, laborious, and eager in getting an estate, and that he will grow rich in proportion to the greatness of his hunger.

Iron.—For one to dream that he sees himself

hurt with iron signifies that he shall receive some damage. To dream that one trades with a stranger in iron signifies to the dreamer losses and misfortune.

Keys.—A key seen in a dream to him who would marry signifieth a good and handsome wife and a good housekeeper. It is cross to a traveller, for it signifieth he shall be put back, and hindered, and not received. It is good for such as would take in hand other men's business.

Kill.—To dream you kill a man signifies assuredness of business; to dream you kill your father is a bad sign; to dream you are killed denotes loss to him who has killed you.

Kite.—To dream of seeing a kite shows you shall be in danger of robbers.

Knives.—For a man to dream he sees knives shows he shall be engaged with some of his friends and acquaintances in a very hot contest and quarrel; but that after a few hot words all shall be pacified, and they shall be good friends again.

Ladder.—The ladder is a sign of travelling; the steps are advancement, but some say they are danger. To dream that you ascend a ladder signifies honour, but to dream that you descend a ladder betokeneth damage.

Lantern.—He that dreams that he sees a lantern with a light in it extinguished or darkened—that signifies unto him sadness, sickness, and poverty.

Light.—When one dreams that he holds a

burning light in his hands in the night it is a good sight, and chiefly to those who are young, for it signifies that they shall prosper in love, accomplish their designs, overcome their enemies, and gain honour and goodwill from all persons. To dream you see a burning light in the hands of another signifies that the mischief done will be discovered and the party punished.

Linen.—To dream you are dressed in clean linen denotes that you will shortly receive some glad tidings; if it is dirty, then it denotes poverty, a prison, and disappointment in love, with the loss of something valuable.

Lion.—If one dreams he combats with a lion, it signifies a quarrel, and that he shall engage with some resolute adversary; if he dreamed he came off victorious, it shall certainly be so.

Logs.—To dream that one is cleaving of logs is a sign that strangers shall come to the house.

Looking, or Looking-glass.—To dream of looking down from high places, or out of windows, or being in a high garret, shows an ambitious mind, curious desires, wandering imagination, and confused thoughts. To dream of looking in a glass, in married folks, betokens children; in young folks, sweethearts.

Lord.—To dream you discourse with a lord or that you go into any place with him signifies honour.

Lost and Losing.—For a woman to dream that she has lost her wedding-ring signifies that she has but small love for her husband; but if she dreams that she has found it again, it is a sign her love is not wholly lost. And if a man dreams of losing his shoes, and then his feet are bare, if he be of a sanguine complexion it signifies he shall meet with reproaches, especially if he dreams it in the first day of the new moon.

Manure.—To dream that man manures or cultivates earth signifies melancholy to those that are not of such a condition; but to labourers it signifies gain and a good crop.

Marry.—To dream that you marry signifies damage, sickness, melancholy, and sometimes death. If a sick person so dream, it is an evident token of death.

Mason.—To dream you build a house or play the mason signifies molestation, loss, sickness, or death, and is a very unhappy dream.

Mountains.—To dream of mountains, valleys, woods, and plains indicates heaviness and fear, troubles; stripes to servants and malefactors; and hurt to the rich. It is always better to cross over them, and not to stay there and slumber by the way.

Mule.—To dream of a mule signifies malice and foolish imaginations.

Music.—To dream you hear melodious music, which is even ready to ravish your ear, signifies that the party dreaming shall suddenly hear some very acceptable news, with which he shall be greatly delighted. But if people dream that they hear harsh, discordant notes and ill-tuned music, it signifies the contrary; and they shall soon meet with such tidings as they do not care to hear.

Nails.—To dream your nails are grown long is very good, and denotes riches, prosperity, and happiness, and great success in love, a good industrious husband or wife, and dutiful children. It also foretells that you will suddenly receive a sum of money that will be of great use to you.

Neck.—To dream of the neck signifies power, honour, riches, and inheritances.

Nettles.—To dream of nettles, and that you sting yourself with them, shows that you will venture hard for what you desire to obtain.

Night-Birds.—To dream of any sort of night-birds, as the owlet, the great owl, bittern, and bat, ominous; and Anselmus Julianus advises those who have such dreams to undertake no business on the day following.

Nightingale.—To dream of this pretty warbler is the forerunner of joyful news, great success in business, of plentiful crops, and of a sweet-tempered lover.

Nosegay.—To dream of gathering and making nosegays is unlucky, showing that your best hopes shall wither as flowers do in a nosegay. To dream of garlands is very good in the spring, but bad in the other seasons.

Nut-Trees.—To dream that you see nut-trees, and that you crack and eat their fruit, signifies riches and content, gained with labour and pains. To dream that you find nuts that have been hid signifies that you will find some treasure.

Oak.—To dream that one sees a stately oak signifies to the dreamer riches, profit, and long life.

Oil.—To dream of being anointed with oil is good for all women, except those who are wicked; but for men it is ill, and signifies shame, except those who are accustomed to use it, as surgeons, painters, oilmen, and the like.

Olive-Tree.—To dream you see an olive-tree with olives denotes peace, delight, concord, liberty, dignity, and fruition of your desires.

Onions.—To dream of these useful vegetables denotes a mixture of good and ill luck. If you are eating them, you will receive some money, recover some lost or stolen thing, or discover some hidden treasure. Your sweetheart will be faithful, but of a cross temper.

Organs.—To dream that you hear the sound of organs signifies joy.

Oysters.—To dream of opening and eating oysters shows great hunger, which the party dreaming shall suddenly sustain; or else that he shall take great pains for his living, as they do that open oysters.

Palm.—If one dreams that he sees or smells the palm, it signifies amity, prosperity, abundance, and good success in his enterprises.

Peaches.—To dream of peaches, bastard peaches, and such kinds of fruit in season, denotes to him that dreams he sees or eats them content, health, and pleasure.

Peas.—To dream of peas well boiled denotes good success and expedition of business.

ANCIENT INTERPRETATIONS

Pictures.—To dream one draws pictures is pleasure without profit.

Plough.—To dream of a plough is good for marriage, courtship, and such-like affairs; but it requireth some time to bring them to perfection.

Precipices.—To dream that one sees great and deep precipices, and that one falls over them, signifies that he that dreams will suffer much injury and hazard of his person, and his goods be in danger by fire.

Queen.—To dream that you see the King or Queen signifies honour, joy, and much prosperity.

Race.—To dream of running a race is good to all except they be sick persons when they dream they come to the end of their race, for it signifies that shortly they shall come to the end of their life.

Rainbow.—To dream you see a rainbow denotes the changing of your present estate and manner of life.

Rice.—To dream of eating rice denotes abundance of instruction.

Sable.—To dream one is in a room hung with sable or mourning shows the person dreaming shall quickly hear of the death of some near relation or very near friend.

Saddle.—To dream you are riding a horse without a saddle signifies poverty, disgrace, and shame to the dreamer.

Silver.—If one dreams he gathers up silver, it signifies damage and loss. To see silver eaten signifies great advantage. To eat silver signifies wrath and anger.

Swimming.—An omen of great social distinction.

Tapestry.—To dream that one makes tapestry signifies joy without any great reason for it.

Vaults.—To dream of being in hollow vaults, deep cellars, or the bottom of deep coal-pits, signifies matching for a widow; for he that marries her shall be a continual drudge, and yet shall never sound the depths of her policies.

Vinegar.—To dream that you drink vinegar signifies sickness.

Walnuts.—To dream that one sees and eats walnuts or hazel-nuts signifies difficulty and trouble.

Wasps.—To dream you are stung by wasps signifies vexation and trouble from envious persons.

Wrestling. — A woman who dreams she wrestles with her husband will certainly bring shame and sorrow into the family. For children to wrestle with men is good. Wrestling in a dream with death denotes a long sickness and lawsuits.

Write.—To dream one writes on paper signifies accusation.

SCIENTIFIC EXPLANATIONS OF THE DREAMING STATE

It may be agreed that there is a good ground for believing that in the dream-state the mind, or soul, or consciousness—whatever we may choose to call it—is enabled to do things that are not possible to it in the ordinary waking state. Modern science supports this view.

In sleep some of the faculties of the mind are still working, though they may bring over to the waking state very few impressions of what has happened. Sleeping allows a freer play to the mental side of the individual. It is well known that if a problem that presents many difficulties has to be worked out, it is quite a usual thing to say, " I will sleep over it."

In the morning many of the difficulties have vanished. Although there is no knowledge of what has happened in many cases, the mind has been at work during sleep, and the problem has been practically straightened out. In hypnotism, which is only a deep sleep produced by artificial means, the mind works very clearly, and shows that it possesses powers far greater than is usually supposed to be the case.

The scientific explanation of this is that the mind may be considered made up of two parts —the ordinary mind, or objective mind, and the inner mind, or subjective mind. It is the inner mind that works principally in sleep, either in ordinary sleep or hypnotic sleep, and that also helps the individual in moments of great danger.

When the body is dulled by sleep or unconsciousness the inner mind has a chance to escape, as it were, from its attention to the affairs of the body. It is released from its chains, and can work more easily.

This is why in moments of great danger, or when death is very near and the body is incapable of action or movement, the mind is able to present itself to persons at a distance. It can and does appear as an apparition or wraith that tries to give a message to some loved one. There are numberless cases of these appearances which have been well testified and must be believed.

It may be thought that this has little to do with dreams. But really it is most important. For if we can establish the fact that the mind may and does sometimes act almost independently of the body in sleep, we shall be able to see that some dreams are real, and may well be perhaps solemn warnings of what is to happen.

And here we have to refer to a very deep issue. All our experience tends to show us that all things happen in a certain order. Nothing really happens accidentally. Everything that does happen has a cause. All that occurs is the direct outcome of something that has happened before. The present, therefore, is the child of the past. The future is just as inevitably the child of the present.

Now, this is a great thing for us to be able to say. For if the future is really caused by the

THE DREAMING STATE

present, we can see the workings of fate—of destiny. The future cannot be otherwise. And the future can be foretold. This is why prophecies are possible. This is why dreams may foretell the future.

Time is a convenient expression only in reality. There is, to the Great Mind, no such thing as time; there is neither past, present, nor future. Everything appears to the Great Architect of the Universe as an ETERNAL NOW.

The links that bind the past, present, and future into one whole are such that there can be no separation into such parts. To the little or ordinary mind of man, to which things are presented with its bodily eyes, those things as they happen *seem* to be so divided.

But to the inner mind there is no such thing as time or space. It is a part of the Great Mind to which there is neither past nor future. The links of the chain are dimly seen, and a glimpse is obtained of what is to come by this inner mind of ours.

And not only is this possible in sleep. There are day-dreams. The musician, the painter, the storyteller, the architect, the sculptor, and the poet, have their dreams, in their ordinary waking state, and their beautiful work is the outcome of it. In some cases the work is actually the result of a real dream. R. L. Stevenson's wonderful story of Dr. Jekyll and Mr. Hyde was a dream.

Artistic creation—the work of the musician or painter, etc.—in the day-dream state is nearly always accomplished while the body is almost wholly at rest. The artist is not conscious of his bodily surroundings. He is living for the moment in a dream-state—in another world: the world of visions. He sees and hears things with the eyes and ears of the inner mind—with that finer sense that is given to the ordinary person only in sleep, and then not too often.

Many of our dreams we cannot recall. We wake in the morning knowing that we have dreamed beautiful things or sorrowful things, but find that we cannot remember them. This means that we have not yet learned to bring them over to our waking state, to be made use of.

But yet they may actually be present to the inner mind as warnings which are acted upon without our actually knowing them. We make decisions to do this or not to do that without quite knowing why we do. But really we have been warned in a dream.

In an earlier part of this chapter it was suggested that most dreaming and seeing of visions was to be attributed to the power of the inner or subjective, unconscious, mind to transcend the limitations of time and space. There are, however, other explanations which are worth attention.

Racial memory, or the stored-up impressions in the mind, which are assumed to be transmitted right down through the ages for countless generations, are said to account for many dreams. When we sleep we are less able to control ourselves than at any other time. It is then that the recollections and remembrances of a long-vanished past surge over us.

THE DREAMING STATE

These dreams are not so much warnings of what is to happen as reconstructions of what has happened. We live over again fragments of the lives of our ancestors in the dim past. We think and act as they did. We see the things they saw. We love, and fear, and hate, as they did.

Often when we wake we are only barely conscious of the strangeness of these dreams. We have lost the sequence, the continuity of the thoughts, and sights, and actions. We just know that we have lived through weird and distressing, or brave and hopeful and gallant times. It is by the great differences we have felt that we have been made aware of the gap between those times and our own.

Still another explanation is that of the influence of spirits. At death, it is suggested, part only of that which we call man—the body, soul, and spirit—dies; the remainder lives on for ever. The surviving individuality — the soul and spirit—perhaps needs to impress some message or warning or other communication upon the living, ordinary world. It takes the opportunity of finding a mind, suitably free in sleep, upon which it endeavours to impress its message.

The dreamer is unconscious of this external influence, and feels and acts in his dream-state as though he was living through this experience himself. If the dream is a vivid one, it will persist and have some real effect in modifying the waking life.

Inspiration is of this type. In our dream-life

we are helped by these discarnate intelligencies in this way. On other occasions, however, it may be that we are tempted and counselled wrongly. The souls who have passed over are not all saints. Many of them are wrong-doers, eager and anxious for the chance of making their influences for evil still effective.

Deprived of a physical vehicle for work on our ordinary plane, they peer and pry till an opportunity is afforded of using another body as the channel for their evil-doing. In sleep we lay off a portion—a goodly portion—of our armour. The enemy is then able to get through the defences.

But we have a remedy for this. Before committing the body to sleep the powers of the mind—the higher powers of the self within—should be roused. A spiritual armour should be donned. An invocation, addressed to the Greatest that we know and honour and love, will clothe the sleeping form with powers of resistance to evil. An appeal for guidance and help, sent to the same quarter, will insure its due effect. We shall sleep in confidence, knowing that protection is afforded and that help and power will flow in to assist and strengthen us.

One other explanation may be suggested for dreams. It is that given by the theory of reincarnation. This theory proposes that the human soul in each body has lived countless lives before. Between each earth life and the next one there is a long rest, for centuries. This body we use now knows nothing of the previous existences of the soul that informs it.

THE DREAMING STATE

One could not expect the suit of clothes that we wore and destroyed last year to know or show signs of anything that happened this year to its successor. But the *man* who wore both would know what happened to each. It is the soul, then, that persists. And it is the soul only that knows.

In sleep the soul is free from the hamperings of the body and its limitations. The soul then knows what happened to it in its previous lives. It lives these over again in recollection. It has glimpses here and there of its past experiences. Some of these are dimly remembered and brought over to the waking consciousness. In other cases the soul, knowing its own immortality, is able to glean and bring back some ideas of its immediate future. It *knows* what is to happen, and tries to warn and guide its gross vehicle aright—to direct it amid the stream of impressions it is receiving minute by minute which distract it and lead it astray.

MODERNISED MEANINGS OF DREAMS

To Dream of—

Acorn—(to see) ill news or slander; (to gather) a legacy.

Almonds—peace and successful enterprise.

Almond-Tree—in business you will profit, and your home-life will be happy.

Altar—good fortune.

Ants—good fortune by change of home.

Ape—strange enemies and deceitfulness.

Apples—(to see) good fortune; (to eat) disappointment.

Apple-Tree—good news will soon reach you.

Artichokes—vexations and troubles, which, however, you will surmount.

Ashes—misfortunes and losses.

Asparagus—good fortune.

Baker—good fortune speedily awaits you.

Balloon—lack of success in business.

Barley—a good omen; riches await you.

Barn—(full) marriage and money; (empty) poverty; (on fire) good fortune.

Bath—(to take one) approaching marriage; (too hot) separation; (too cold) sorrow.

Beans — your actions will be questioned; (green) losses await you.

Bear — persecution; (to kill) victory over enemies.

MODERNISED MEANINGS

Bed—(strange) security.
Bees—a good dream; (stung by) unsuccessful lawsuit.
Beggar—unexpected help.
Bells—misfortune.
Benediction—an unexpected and unwelcome wedding.
Birds—a journey; (singing) gain and success in undertakings.
Biscuits—a fine and prosperous journey.
Bishop—sudden death of a friend or relative.
Blackbird—deceit and slander.
Blind man—deceit where least expected.
Boar—(to chase a wild one) unsuccessful efforts; (to be chased) separation.
Boiled Meat—sufferings.
Bottles—(empty) illness; (wine) prosperity; (upset) domestic troubles.
Bouquet—(to carry) marriage; (to throw away) separation.
Bread—good fortune; (white) constant affection.
Breaking—(things) a bad omen.
Brigand—dangers are in store, but you will surmount them.
Brook—(clear) constant friends; (troubled) family troubles.
Bull—(gored) injury from influential person; (to kill one) suffering; (two bulls fighting) brotherly love.
Burden—(carrying) you will depend upon others for help.
Burial—news of a wedding.
Burial-Ground—tidings of sorrow.

Burning—(houses) a good omen; better fortune for all who witness it.
Burns—(yourself) good fortune.
Butter—surprises; (to make) legacy.
Butterfly—domestic troubles.
Cabbage—health and long life.
Cakes—you will receive a very welcome visitor.
Calf—speedy good fortune.
Camel — prosperity; (a caravan) squandered wealth.
Canary—death of a friend.
Candles — (lighted) a good omen; (extinguished) a funeral; (lighting one) good fortune.
Cards—(playing at) approaching marriage; (to see) quarrels and difficulties.
Carpenter—difficulties will soon be arranged to the satisfaction of everyone.
Cat—(seeing) treachery; (bitten by) misfortune; (caressing) false friends.
Cauliflower—illness and inconstancy.
Caves—losses and afflictions.
Chain—joined interests which will result satisfactorily; (to break) danger and annoyance.
Cheese—difficulties overcome.
Cherries—good health; (to gather) a deceitful woman; (to eat) love.
Chess—(playing) you will encounter difficulties in your business.
Chestnuts—domestic affliction.
Chestnut-Tree—profitable undertakings.
Chicken — constant friends; (to kill one) monetary difficulties.
Child—happiness in store; (running) business troubles.

Church — inheritance; (to pray in) deceit; (to speak in) quarrels at home.

Cobbler — misfortunes that will be well borne, with good fortune to follow.

Cock — success and good fortune; (fighting) expensive amusements.

Cockchafer — business troubles, and perhaps misfortune.

Coffin — disagreements and losses.

Corn — riches.

Corpse — news of the sick; (drowned) estrangement.

Counterpane — (torn) an accident to one in your house.

Cow — (one) good luck; (herd) prosperity.

Crab — beware of the law.

Crocodile — great dangers.

Cross — Grief.

Crow — unsuccessful love affair.

Cuckoo — misfortune; (to hear one) mourning.

Cucumber — serious illness.

Currants — (red) good friends; (white) success; (black) betrayal.

Cypress — bad news of one dear to you.

Dancing — money will come to you; (to watch it) you will receive a visit from an unexpected source.

Dead — (to dream of the) news of the living; (to speak to) long life; (to touch or kiss) sorrow.

Dentist — sickness and ill-health.

Diamonds — (to find) trouble; (to sell) danger.

Digging — good fortune if ground is good and dry; (finding money) good fortune if much.

Ditch—financial disaster; you will lose all.
Doctor—a good omen; fortune and health; a rise in life.
Dog—(howling) danger; (to lose one) misfortune; (to hunt with one) hopefulness; (to play with one) suffering from former wastefulness; (two fighting) false friends.
Donkey—quarrelsome friends; (asleep) security; (braying) dishonour; (heavily laden) profit; (to shoe one) hard and useless labour.
Dove—happiness in domestic affairs.
Draughts—(playing) your affections are being trifled with; beware.
Dress—(white) good and kind friends; (black) death of a friend or relative; (torn) misfortune.
Duck or Goose—(flying) increase of fortune; (swimming) plenty.
Dust—(blinded by) business difficulties and losses in family circle.
Dwarf—difficulties to be encountered.
Eagle—(flying) ambition and gratified fortune; (dead) loss.
Eclipse—(sun) misfortune; (moon) success.
Eels—(alive) hard work; (dead) triumph over enemies.
Eggs—wealth.
Elephant—future dignity; (to feed) someone will do you a very good turn.
Embroidery—affection that is returned.
Escape—(inability to) trouble will overtake you; (successful) you will overcome your dangers.
Falcon—good fortune.

OF DREAMS

Fan—look before you leap.
Fatigue—(yourself) success in business.
Fawn—dangers to come soon.
Feast—trouble in store.
Feathers—(white) friendship and happiness; (black) losses.
Fence—(climbing) a sudden rise in life; (creeping under) a warning to avoid shady transactions.
Fields—family joy and good health.
Figs—(dried) rejoicings; (green) hope; (to eat) ill fortune to be expected.
Fire—quarrels; (small) good news.
Fish—success; (to catch them) your friends are false; (dead) quarrels and disappointments.
Fleas—weariness of life; (to kill one) success over enemies.
Flies—good fortune excites jealousy.
Floating—(on water) good fortune and speedy success; (sinking) look out for reverses of fortune.
Flowers—happiness; (to gather) abiding friendship; (to cast away) quarrels.
Flute—(to hear) news of a birth.
Footman—unexpected enemies.
Forest—misfortune and disgrace.
Fountain—a good dream; prosperity and health.
Fox—(killed) good; (petted) danger; (to see one) secret enemies.
Friend—quarrels made up.
Fright—to be interpreted by its contrary.
Frogs—deceitfulness; (hopping) vexation and annoyance; (catching) good fortune.

Funeral—a legacy unexpected.
Funeral-Service—inheritance.
Garden—good fortune in store; (trim) money; (badly kept) misfortune.
Garland—anticipated pleasures will be realised.
Garlic—the fair sex will cause you trouble.
Gauze—concealed feelings.
Ghost—(if frightened by) bad, great difficulties; (otherwise) good fortune.
Gift—(woman) spite; (man) danger.
Gloves—transient joy.
Goat—(white) good fortune; (black) illness; (on high places) riches.
Grapes—(to eat) good fortune; (to throw away) loss, dangers, vexations; (to tread on them) plenty.
Grasshopper—loss of harvest.
Grave—(filled up) a good omen; (open) bad news.
Grinding—(corn) good fortune; (coffee) trouble at home; (pepper) sickness and sorrow.
Guitar—(to play) scandal or ill news.
Hail—affliction and sorrow.
Ham—joy and pleasure.
Hands—(tied) trouble.
Hare—(running) fortune leaving you.
Hay—happiness and success; (to mow it) sorrow.
Hen—substantial profit; (cackling) immense fortune; (with chicks) doubtful fortune; (laying eggs) gain.
Herbs—good fortune will be yours; (to eat) disappointment.
Hiding—ill news will soon reach you.

Holly—vexation and disagreements.
Honey—profitable enterprises.
Horse—success; (black) partial success only; (white) very good fortune; (to shoe one) very lucky.
Horseman—a dangerous journey.
Ice—false friends.
Ink—(spilled) separation and losses.
Journey—a change of circumstances as the dream may indicate.
Kiss—awaking affection.
Kitchen—visit from relatives.
Knives—beware of hatred which may afflict you seriously.
Labourer—increased wealth.
Ladder—(climbing) good; (dizziness) bad.
Lambs (to find one) success at law; (in fields) peacefulness and health; (to eat) sorrow.
Lame Man—business difficulties.
Lamps—showiness.
Landscape—great good fortune.
Larks—you will be soon richer than you are.
Laughter—grief and pain.
Laurel—pleasure and profitable undertakings.
Lawyer—the marriage of a friend.
Leech—fortunate friends and happiness await you.
Leeks—perseverance in your project will bring its reward in due time.
Leopard—dangers and travels.
Letters—(to receive) good news from abroad.
Lettuce—misfortune is awaiting you.
Lightning—a love squabble.
Linen—an inheritance or good fortune.

Lion—prospective honour; (captive) unfailing friendship; (to kill one) good fortune, success; (to overcome one) great success; (to hear one roar) grievous danger from jealous persons.
Lioness—a good dream.
Lion's Cub—protection and friendship.
Lizards—treachery is afoot.
Luggage — (travelling with) difficulties and dangers.
Mackerel—Deceit and evil tidings.
Magic—good fortune awaits you.
Mantle—a device is afoot to deceive you.
Marriage—affliction and danger.
Medlars — your enjoyment will cease and troubles ensue.
Melon—satisfaction.
Mice — unsuccessful undertakings; dangers from friends.
Mills—inheritance of fortune; you will inherit a legacy.
Mirror—false friends; (broken) death of a relative.
Money—losses in business; (to find it) misfortune; (to change it) troubles to come.
Moneylender—ill fortune.
Moon — requited love; (shining) continued enjoyment; (clouded) illness, danger to a loved one; (full) wealth; (new) awakened affection; (waning) deceit.
Mountains—a good dream; (climbing) good fortune will reward you.
Mourning—invitation to festivities; happiness awaits you.
Mud—an omen of good fortune.

OF DREAMS

Muff—beware of inconstancy.
Mule—bad news of lawsuit; (riding) will never be married, or childless.
Music—pleasures in store.
Myrtle—a love avowal.
Navigating a Vessel—you will take a long journey.
Necklace—jealousy and quarrels.
Needles—disappointments in love.
Negro—spiteful friends.
Nest—good fortune and prosperity.
Nightingale—happy marriage; joy.
Noises—your position will be influenced by someone dying.
Nurse—a good omen.
Nuts—your wishes will be gratified.
Oak—prosperity and long life; (felled) losses.
Old man—good fortune.
Old woman—scandal.
Olives—a good omen.
Onions—(peeling) family troubles; (eating) unexpected good fortune.
Opera—enjoyment which is not without its penalties.
Orange-Blossom—a near marriage.
Oranges—amusement; (to eat) pleasures to come.
Organ—(solemn music) sickness and family troubles.
Owl—(flying) beware of your secrets.
Oysters—unreasonable feasting.
Painter—a good dream.
Painting—domestic affliction.
Palm—you will be successful in your enterprises, and confound those who oppose you.

48 MODERNISED MEANINGS

Parent—success for one you hold dear.
Parrot—dangerous neighbours.
Pastry—sickness and pain.
Peaches—happiness for yourself and those dear to you.
Peacock—doubtful position in life; (spreading its tail) vanity and pride.
Pearls—sorrow; (to thread) grief and distress.
Pears—deceit; (to eat) news of a death; (to gather) coming happiness.
Peas—success.
Pens, Paper—letters or tidings of friends.
Pheasant—good fortune; (to carry one) honour awaits you.
Pig—good fortune coming.
Pigeon—content and success.
Pilgrim—successful future.
Pine—there is danger near.
Pins—squabbles.
Play—(seeing one) happiness and good fortune; (to take part) lack of success.
Plums—enjoyment and ease; (green) constant friends; (dried) difficulties.
Policeman—family troubles which will soon be settled.
Pomegranate—a happy augury; honours will come to you.
Porcupine—business difficulties.
Porter—slander and annoyance.
Postman—news of friends.
Precipice—dangers; (to fall) beware of a false friend.
Priest—settlement of quarrels.
Procession—steadfast affection.

Property—(to see) this means you will be disappointed in your hopes.
Quarrel—reunited friends.
Rabbit—(warren) costly enjoyments; (to see rabbits) increase of family.
Rain—a legacy or present.
Rainbow—estrangement.
Ram—misfortune.
Rats—enemies; (white) triumph over enemies.
Raven—a bad omen; (flying) news of a death; (croaking) sadness.
Reading—your project is a dangerous one; give it up.
Reaper—the simple life for you.
Reptiles—a subtle enemy.
Ribbons—pleasure and gaiety and foolish expenditure.
Ring—approaching wedding.
Rings—the consummation of love.
Rival—domestic affliction and sorrow.
River—(to fall in) envious enemies; (to jump in) business disturbances and family troubles.
Roast Meat—affectionate greetings.
Rock—annoyance; (to surmount) overcoming dangers.
Room—(strange) you will accomplish your designs.
Roses—always good; (full blown) good fortune and happiness; (faded) success with a spice of danger.
Rue—domestic difficulties.
Sailor—news from abroad.
Salmon—deception; (to eat) family troubles.
Salt—good fortune and wisdom.

Satin or Silk—profitable business.
Sausages—domestic troubles; (to make) illness.
Scissors—you have enemies who will try to steal a march on you.
Sea—a long but prosperous journey.
Sermon—approaching languor and indisposition.
Serpent—ingratitude; (many-headed) temptations.
Sheep—prosperity and happiness.
Shepherd—a bad omen.
Ship—realisation of best hopes; (in danger) very good fortune.
Shipwreck—a dangerous time awaits you.
Shoes—fortunate enterprise.
Singing—troubles will come soon, but be over as speedily.
Skeleton—vexation and domestic troubles.
Sky—happiness; (clouds) misfortune approaching; (clear) serene life.
Smoke—flimsy success.
Snails—intemperance and inconstancy.
Snow—good harvest.
Soldier—fighting or quarrels.
Soles—misfortune and vexation.
Sparrow-hawk—beware of your enemies, they are conspiring against you.
Spider—good fortune; (to kill one) enjoyment; (spinning) much money to come to you.
Stag—a profitable investment; (to chase one) losses in business; (to kill one) malicious acquaintances.
Stars—(shooting) death of a relative.
Storks—a promise of ill tidings.
Storm—dangers and difficulties.

OF DREAMS

Stranger—news of a lost friend.
Straw—misfortune and losses.
Strawberries—unhoped-for success.
Sun—(rising) profits; (setting) losses; (clouded) bad news; (bright) good news.
Supper—news of a birth.
Swallow—successful enterprise; (nest) happiness; (to enter the house) constant friends.
Swans—a good omen; riches.
Swords—bad news.
Taffeta—wealth that will bring no satisfaction.
Tea—enjoyment.
Tears—joy and pleasure.
Theatre—sorrow caused by losses of money and of friends.
Thimble—your occupation will be bettered.
Thirst—if you appease it with good water, the omen is good; if otherwise, the reverse.
Thistles—quarrels which may be avoided.
Thorns—disappointments in store; (to be hurt) money troubles.
Thunder—danger.
Tiger—if you escape, good; but beware of great danger if caught.
Toads—you will be subjected to annoyance, but emerge triumphant.
Tortoise or Turtle—long life and success.
Tower—(ascending one) reverses in fortune.
Travelling—(through forest) obstacles which you will overcome; (over hills) good fortune in store, but not easily accomplished.
Trees—(in leaf) good; (destroyed by storm) family troubles; (leafless) deception; (cut down) losses; (to climb) better fortune.
Trout—your troubles will vanish.

Trumpet—(to hear) sorrow and loss; (to blow) your fortune will improve.
Tunnel—trouble in store, but it will soon pass.
Turkey—stupidity and intemperance.
Turnips—disappointment and vexation.
Turtle-Doves—affection to be bestowed.
Unfortunate—(being so) care will bring success.
Unknown person—sudden return of a long-lost one.
Valley—sickness of a temporary nature.
Veal—certain good fortune.
Vegetables—unrewarded labour; (to gather) quarrels; (to eat) loss in business.
Veil—news of a wedding; (black) separation.
Velvet—gain and good fortune.
Vinegar—useless toil.
Vintage—successful business operations and affection rewarded.
Violets—success in enterprise; (out of season) newly awakened affection.
Vision—danger to the person who appears to you.
Voice—(to hear) the reverse of what it implies: if cheerful, then sorrow is to come; if sad, then joy may be expected.
Vulture—dangerous enemies; (to kill) conquest of misfortune; (to see one devouring its prey) your troubles will cease and fortune smile upon you.
Wading—(muddy water) misfortune; (clear water) a good omen—fortune will smile on you.
Walls—dangerous enterprises and lack of success; (easy descent from) success in business.
Wasps—dangerous enemies.

Watch—a journey by land.
Water—(drinking) a bad omen; (to fall into) reconciliation; (bathing) misfortune and disappointments.
Water-Carrier—money increases.
Waves—you must be prepared to fight for fortune.
Weasel—beware of those who would appear to befriend you without reason.
Weeding—happiness and good fortune will be yours.
Well—(to draw water) success and profit; (to fall in) danger that can scarcely be avoided.
Wheat—riches will be yours.
Whirlwind—beware of dangerous reports.
Wind—a presage of a good time coming.
Window—you will be annoyed and distressed by slander.
Wings—bad dream.
Wolf—enmity; (to kill) success; (to pursue) dangers overcome; (pursued by) dangers.
Woodcutter—your efforts will not result in much profit.
Workhouse—a big legacy to come soon.
Workman—your enterprises will bring great profit.
Workshop—a sign of good fortune.
Worms—danger of infectious diseases.
Writing—you will receive good news from an unexpected quarter.
Yarn—you will receive a fine present from an unexpected quarter.
Yawning—energy will be necessary if you are to succeed.
Zebra—disagreement with friends.

OMENS: ANCIENT AND MODERN

An appeal to antiquity is usually a safe ground for a basis. How, then, have omens been regarded in past ages? It is found that almost the earliest records that are extant to-day—the Babylonian and Assyrian tablets—regard omens as of very great importance. In India, too, where the records of the early ages of civilisation go back to the dim past, omens are considered of great significance.

Later, in Greece, the home of the greatest and highest culture and civilisation, we find, too, omens regarded very seriously. To-day there are vast numbers of persons in all climes and degrees of intellection who place reliance upon omens.

That there is some good ground for belief in some omens seems indisputable. Whether this has arisen as the result of experience, by the following of some particular event close upon the heels of signs observed, or whether it has been an intuitive science, in which prevision has been used to afford an interpretation, is not quite clear. It seems idle to attempt to dismiss the whole thing as mere superstition, wild guessing, or abject credulity, as some try to do, with astrology and alchemy also, and other occult sciences; the fact remains that omens have, in numberless instances, given good warnings.

OMENS

To say that these are just coincidences is to beg the question. For the universe is governed by law. Things happen because they must, not because they may. There is no such thing as accident or coincidence. We may not be able to see the steps and the connections. But they are there all the same.

In the official guide to the British Museum of the Babylonian and Assyrian antiquities the following appears in relation to Table Case H. in the Nineveh Gallery: "By means of omen tablets the Babylonian and Assyrian priests from time immemorial predicted events which they believed would happen in the near or in the remote future. They deduced these omens from the appearance and actions of animals, birds, fish, and reptiles; from the appearance of the entrails of sacrificial victims; from the appearance and condition of human and animal offspring at birth; from the state and condition of various members of the human body."

Other signs were deduced from the symptoms of sick men; from the events or actions of a man's life; from dreams and visions; from the appearance of a man's shadow; from fire, flame, light, or smoke; from the state and condition of cities and their streets, of fields, marshes, rivers, and lands. From the appearances of the stars and planets, of eclipses, meteors, shooting stars, the direction of winds, the form of clouds, from thunder and lightning and other weather incidents, they were able to forecast happenings. A whole host of tablets are devoted to these predictions.

It is conceivable that many of these omens should have found their way into Greece. It is not unreasonable to believe that India may have derived her knowledge of omens from Babylonia; or, indeed, it may have been the other way about. The greatest scholars to-day are divided in their opinions as to which really is the earlier civilisation.

But the point to be made here is that in all parts of the world—in quarters where we may be certain that no trace of Grecian, Indian, or Babylonian science or civilisation has appeared—there are to be found systems of prediction by omens.

This may be accounted for in two ways. One that in all races as they grow up, so to speak, there is the same course of evolution of ideas and superstition which to many appears childish. The other explanation seems to be the more reasonable one, if we believe, as we are forced to do, that omens do foretell—that all peoples, all races, accumulate a record, oral or written, of things which have happened more or less connected with things which seemed to indicate them. In course of time this knowledge appears to consolidate. It gets generally accepted as true. And then it is handed on from generation to generation. Often with the passage of years it gets distorted and wrested away from its original meaning.

It would be difficult to attempt to classify omens. Many large books have been written on the subject. Many more will be written of the beliefs of the various races. The best that

ANCIENT AND MODERN

can be offered here will be a little selection from one or other of the varied sources. In Greece sneezing was a good omen. It was considered, too, a proof of the truth of what was said at the moment by the sneezer.

A tingling in the hand denoted the near manipulation of money, a ringing in the ears that news will soon be received. The number of sneezes then became a sign for more definite results. The hand which tingled, either right or left, indicated whether it were to be paid or received. The particular ear affected was held to indicate good or evil news. Other involuntary movements of the body were also considered of prime importance.

Many omens are derived from the observation of various substances dropped into a bowl of water. In Babylon oil was used. To-day in various countries melted lead, wax, or the white of an egg, is used. From the shapes which result, the trade or occupation of a future husband, the luck for the year, and so on, are deduced in the folk practices of modern Europe. Finns use stearine and melted lead, Maygars lead, Russians wax, Danes lead and egg, and the northern counties of England egg.

Bird omens were the subject of very serious study in Greece. It has been thought that this was because in the early mythology of Greece some of their gods and goddesses were believed to have been birds. Birds, therefore, were particularly sacred, and their appearances and movements were of profound significance. The principal birds for signs were the raven, the crow, the heron, wren, dove, woodpecker, and kingfisher, and all the birds of prey, such as the hawk, eagle, or vulture, which the ancients classed together (W. R. Halliday, "Greek Divination"). Many curious instances, which were fulfilled, of bird omens are related by the Rev. F. G. Lee in "The Other World." A number of families have traditions about the appearance of a white bird in particular.

In the ancient family of Ferrers, of Chartley Park, in Staffordshire, a herd of wild cattle is preserved. A tradition arose in the time of Henry III. that the birth of a parti-coloured calf is a sure omen of death, within the same year, to a member of the Lord Ferrers family. By a noticeable coincidence, a calf of this description has been born whenever a death has happened of late years in this noble family (*Staffordshire Chronicle*, July, 1835). The falling of a picture or a statue or bust of the individual is usually regarded as an evil omen. Many cases are cited where this has been soon followed by the death of the person.

It would be easy to multiply instances of this sort of personal omen or warning. The history and traditions of our great families are saturated with it. The predictions and omens relating to the luck of Edenhall, to the Tichborne family, and others, recur at once; and from these it may be inferred that beneath the more popular beliefs there is enough fire and truth to justify the smoke that is produced, and to reward some of the faith that is placed in the modern dream-books and the books of fate and the interpretations of omens.

OMENS

Bees are weather-wise. They do not venture far from the hive if a storm is near.

Birthdays.—One old rhyme runs:

> " Sunday's child is full of grace,
> Monday's child is full in the face,
> Tuesday's child is solemn and sad,
> Wednesday's child is merry and glad,
> Thursday's child is inclined to thieving,
> Friday's child is free in giving,
> Saturday's child works hard for his living.'

There is, however, another version as follows .

> " Monday's child is fair of face,
> Tuesday's child is full of grace,
> Wednesday's child is full of woe,
> Thursday's child has far to go,
> Friday's child is loving and giving,
> Saturday's child works hard for its living;
> But a child that's born on the Sabbath-day
> Is handsome and wise and loving and gay."

Candle.—A spark on the wick of a candle means a letter for the one who first sees it. A big glow like a parcel means money coming to you.

Clothes.—To put on clothes the wrong way out is a sign of good luck; but you must not alter them, or the luck will change.

Crickets.—A lucky omen. It foretells money coming to you. They should not be disturbed.

Death-Watch.—A clicking in the wall by this little insect is regarded as evil, but it does not necessarily mean a death; possibly only some sickness.

Ears.—You are being talked about if your ear tingles. Some say, "right for spite, left for love." Others reverse this omen. If you think of the person, friend, or acquaintance who is likely to be talking of you, and mention the name aloud, the tingling will cease if you say the right one.

Fruit Stones or Pips.—Think of a wish first, and then count your stones or pips. If the number is even, the omen is good. If odd, the reverse is the case.

Knives crossed are a bad omen. If a knife or fork or scissors falls to the ground and sticks in the floor you will have a visitor.

Ladybirds betoken visitors.

Magpies.—One, bad luck; two, good luck; three, a wedding; four, a birth.

Marriage.—A maid should not wear colours; a widow never white. Happy omens for brides are sunshine and a cat sneezing.

May.—"Marry in May, and you'll rue the day."

New Moon on a Monday signifies good luck and good weather. The new moon seen for the first time over the right shoulder offers the chance for a wish to come true.

Nightingale.—Lucky for lovers if heard before the cuckoo.

Owls.—Continuous hooting of owls in your trees is said to be an omen of ill-health.

Pigs.—To meet a sow coming towards you is good ; but if she turns away, the luck flies.

Rabbits.—A rabbit running across your path is said to be unlucky.

Salt spilled means a quarrel. This may be avoided by throwing a pinch over the left shoulder.

Shoes.—The right shoe is the best one to put on first.

Shooting Stars.—If you wish, while the star is still moving, your wish will come true.

Singing before breakfast, you'll cry before night.

Spiders.—The little red spider is the money spider, and means good fortune coming to you. It must not be disturbed. Long-legged spiders are also forerunners of good fortune.

Washing Hands.—If you wash your hands in the water just used by another, a quarrel may be expected, unless you first make the sign of the cross over the water.

YOUR FORTUNE IN THE TEACUP

A very old method of telling fortunes is to interpret the figures formed in the teacup from tea-leaves or coffee-grounds. Tea gives always the best indications, and is most generally used. After the cup of tea has been drunk, and there is only a little remaining at the bottom, the cup should be turned round three times by the handle, with a swinging movement, in the direction the hands of a clock take. This spreads the leaves and grounds well over the cup. The teacup should then be turned upside down to drain away the moisture.

Careful notice should now be taken of all the shapes and figures formed inside the cup. These should be viewed from different positions, so that their meaning becomes clear. It is not always easy at first to see what the shape really is, but after looking at it carefully it becomes plainer. The different shapes and figures in the cup must be taken together in a general reading. Bad indications will be balanced by good ones; some good ones will be strengthened by others, and so on.

Anchor means, at the top, and clear, love and constancy; if cloudy, the reverse must be read. An anchor at the bottom of the cup means fruitful business.

Beasts, other than dogs, foretell misfortune.

Birds are good.

Circles represent money. They mean that the person whose fortune is read may expect to receive money or presents. If the circles are connected by lines, this means delay.

Clover.—A good sign. At the top of the cup, good fortune quickly. As it nears the bottom, it will mean that it is more or less distant.

Coffin.—Long sickness, or even news of a death.

Cross.—A cross is a sign of a death.

Crown.—A crown signifies honour.

Crown and Cross signifies good fortune resulting from a death.

Dog.—At the top, faithful friends; in the middle, they are untrustworthy. A dog at the bottom means secret enemies.

Fish.—Good news from over the sea.

Heart.—Surrounded by dots, signifies the receipt of money and consequent happiness; a ring near it betokens approaching marriage.

Heavenly Bodies.—Sun, moon, and stars signify happiness and success.

Human Figures generally are good, and denote love and marriage.

Letter.—A letter signifies news. If unclouded, good; surrounded by dots, money; but if fixed about by clouds, bad news or loss of money.

Lily.—At the top, foretells a happy marriage; at the bottom, anger or strife.

Man signifies a speedy visitor. If the arm is held out, he brings a present. If figure is very clear, he is dark; if indistinct, he is of light complexion.

Mountains are both good and bad.

Oblong Figures.—Family squabbles.

Ring.—A ring means marriage; and if a letter can be found near it, this is the initial of the future spouse. If clouds are near the ring, an unhappy marriage; if all is clear about it, the contrary. A ring right at the bottom means that the wedding will not take place.

Snakes are a sign of bad omen. Great caution is needed to ward off misfortune.

Squares.—Comfort and peace.

Straight Line.—A journey.

Straight Lines are an indication of peace, happiness, and long life.

Trees.—Restoration to health, if one only; several together and clear, evil that may be avoided. Trees wide apart and clear are a good omen.

Triangle.—An unexpected legacy.

Twisted Figures.—Disturbances and vexation; grievances if there are many such figures.

Wavy Lines.—If long and waved, denote losses and vexations. The importance of the lines depends upon the number of them and if heavy or light.

PALMISTRY

CONTENTS

	PAGE
PREFACE	9
INTRODUCTION	11
GENERAL PRINCIPLES	18
OF HANDS IN GENERAL	27
OF LINES AND THEIR CHARACTERISTICS	34

PRINCIPAL LINES

1. LIFE, HEART AND HEAD	42
2. FATE, FORTUNE AND HEALTH	52

THE MOUNTS

1. JUPITER, SATURN, APOLLO, MERCURY	55
2. MARS, MOON AND VENUS	59

CONCLUSIONS	62

ILLUSTRATIONS

		PAGE
I.	GENERAL DIAGRAM LINES	17
II.	THE MOUNTS	23
III.	LEFT AND RIGHT HANDS COMPARED	29
IV.	BREAKS, SQUARES AND STARS	35
V.	FINGERS: SQUARE AND POINTED	43
VI.	FINGERS: SPATULATE AND CONIC	49
VII.	A MIXED HAND AND FINGER JOINTS	57

PREFACE

IT may come as a surprise to some persons that there are quite a number of large books on the subject of Palmistry. These are devoted to an analysis of its principles, and then to the practical application of these principles by way of illustration. To the authors and publishers of some of these volumes the present writer would here offer his acknowledgments for suggestion in mode of treatment and in a lesser degree for material.

Mrs. Robinson's volume, "The Graven Palm," published by Edward Arnold, is one of these. Cheiro's "Language of the Hand," and "Palmistry for All," published by Herbert Jenkins, are others. Mention must also be made of the large volume, with 800 illustrations, by W. G. Benham, published by G. P. Putnam's Sons, "The Laws of Scientific Hand Reading." Many years' patient investigation is embodied in this book and the subject is treated most exhaustively. Each of these books may be recommended to those who desire a more detailed treatment of the subject than could possibly be given in a little volume at the modest price of ninepence.

But within the limits of the space available it is hoped that a fair presentation of the case for the significance of the art has been made, and that the reader will be able to obtain enough detail to read his own palm and perhaps get a little enjoyment out of his endeavours to read the palms of such of his friends who will submit to his pretensions.

JAMES WARD.

INTRODUCTION

In the minds of very many *superior* persons palmistry is usually associated with a species of clever humbug by which fools can be easily persuaded to part with their money. It must be admitted that these superior persons are usually those to whom everything that fails to fall within their own narrow range of experience is something to be derided as impossible or untrue—if not both. Anything that savours of the mysterious, or of the occult, is synonymous, to them, with charlatanism.

These persons are perfectly convinced, for example, that there can be nothing in clairvoyance, telepathy and psychometry. And this, forsooth, because neither of them have fallen ripe into their hands, ready made and perfect in all their details. If told of occurrences that are really only explicable on the understanding that clairvoyance, telepathy, and psychometry are facts of experience, they merely shrug their shoulders and think they have closed the case for the prosecution by the one word "coincidence."

It might give them pause, if they would think for a moment, of the impossibility of coincidence or accident. If they had any conception of the universe it could only be of a chaos—a contradiction in terms really.

Since the very idea underlying the notion of a universe at all is an order of nature, moving in a co-ordinated progression. In this there is room neither for accident nor coincidence. Things happen because they must—not because they may, or may not, as the case may be.

Our whole life is ordered and run on the conception that there is a law of causation. Each event is linked to some precedent cause. Each event is the effect of that cause operating on lines, or by laws, that we are patiently investigating and slowly ascertaining. When the people of these islands died by the hundred thousand, in the Dark Ages of the Black Death, it was thought to be a visitation of God, to arrest which man was powerless. To-day we overhaul our sources of water supply and exterminate the rats which carry the disease germs.

Wireless telegraphy was an unbelievable wonder until it was actually an accomplished fact. Now we regard it as little more mysterious or marvellous than writing or speaking.

Telepathy has been investigated and found to be no more wonderful, and dependent in fact upon the same laws of etheric vibration.

Aviation was considered impossible until it was actually achieved. Now our field commanders in the war zones use it to determine the movements of the enemy and to foretell his possible points of attack.

In the latter case it would be called intelligent anticipation if the enemy commander, taking into consideration those movements he saw, or had reported to him, was enabled to frustrate the attack afterwards made. The commander has "put two and two together and made four."

He was guided in his deductions by the recognition of the law of causation. He anticipated intelligently, by the signs he had observed, that certain things would follow as a matter of course.

The future is the child of the present. We form the future as we move and live and think to-day. Past, present and future are bound up in one indissoluble "NOW." There is really no *maybe* about the future. It is the inevitable outcome of the doings of to-day.

Man's course is determined just as the orbits or the planets are determined. If we could know *all* the causes that are operating to-day in and around any one life we could say with certainty just what would happen.

But as it is impossible to say even what a few of the causes are which may give effect to the future, the latter is, perhaps, wisely hidden from us almost in its entirety. Yet within reason we can determine the future. We do so momentarily and from day to day.

And, although our anticipations are not always intelligent, and do not always work out as we should desire, still we work on the assumption that the future will be as we desire it to be. We try to shape it to our ends. And for this purpose we endeavour to find out what are the possibilities of the future, so that we may make allowances for these and modify them it may be.

Now, Palmistry is reputed to be one of these aids

in discovering the future course of events. Its professors maintain that within fairly broad lines a clear indication can be given of the general fate and fortune of the individual who submits his palm to their examination. It may be as well, therefore, to see what is really claimed for the art, and on what grounds.

Palmistry, first of all, may be considered under three aspects, as cheirognomy, cheiroscopy, and cheiromancy. The words are derived from the Greek, and all have the common root *cheir* (χείρ), the hand.

But whilst the first deals with the formation of the hand and its digits, the second refers to the classification of the knowledge respecting these and its lines, and the third only deals with prophecy, or the fate as revealed by the hand.

Like most arts, Palmistry has a very definite past. It is not the discovery and practice of yesterday; for Palmistry is thousands of years old. It was known and practised long ago in Chaldea, India, Egypt, and Greece. The very terms we employ to describe it, see above, are descended from the Greeks.

Certain it is that amongst some of these ancient peoples Palmistry enjoyed a very high reputation, and numbered amongst its devotees the most intellectual of their ages. Kings and princes sought its aid to discover what the future held in store for them.

It is, then, on this account of its long practice, that so much lore has grown up around the subject and so many trials have been made and possible errors corrected. Beginning first, perhaps, in observation of certain formations of the hand, and certain curious markings in the palms, some daring speculator arose who made generalisations connecting the two.

These would not be difficult. For it is evident that as the creases in a man's clothes, and the shininess of some part will in a measure indicate whether his occupation be mainly sedentary, so, too, it will be easily ascertained that a hard, calloused palm is the result of much labour.

Such things, however, are hardly the indications of which Palmistry proper takes cognisance. A Sherlock Holmes would deduce, from a casual observation of the hands, many things which would help him in his investigations. He would argue from effects to causes, and so connect up motives. The basis of his deductions would be material facts, of which he possessed an almost unlimited stock. Without such facts to go upon he would have been quite powerless.

This is where we see the connection. Palmistry, too, has its stock of facts. These are not only extremely great in number and wide in scope, but they are continually being revised and added to. Each fresh exponent has a vast amount of material to work upon and he adds his quota. In the case of Mr. Benham, whose book is referred to in the preface, this author spent many years in accumulating a vast stock of material. Then, with this to go upon, he began to compare and classify and finally to deduce his principles. In fact, the author states that his intention was to produce a book that should be scientific in the best sense of the word. He desired to get as far away as possible from the idea of the occult or mysterious. His view was that Palmistry might in time become one of the exact sciences, just as geology or geography has become.

And herein lies the firmest foundation for those who wish conscientiously to study Palmistry—an open mind. They must be prepared to devote some little time and concentration to an appreciation of the mass of facts upon which its principles have been erected, and from which they have been extracted. They cannot expect to find in Palmistry what is universally denied elsewhere—a royal road to the art.

For those, on the other hand, who are willing to accept the evidence—which is offered in the books previously mentioned—who "will take it as read," this little work will be found no doubt of considerable use in presenting them with a sketch, the cream of the subject, which they can easily apply for simple and broad results.

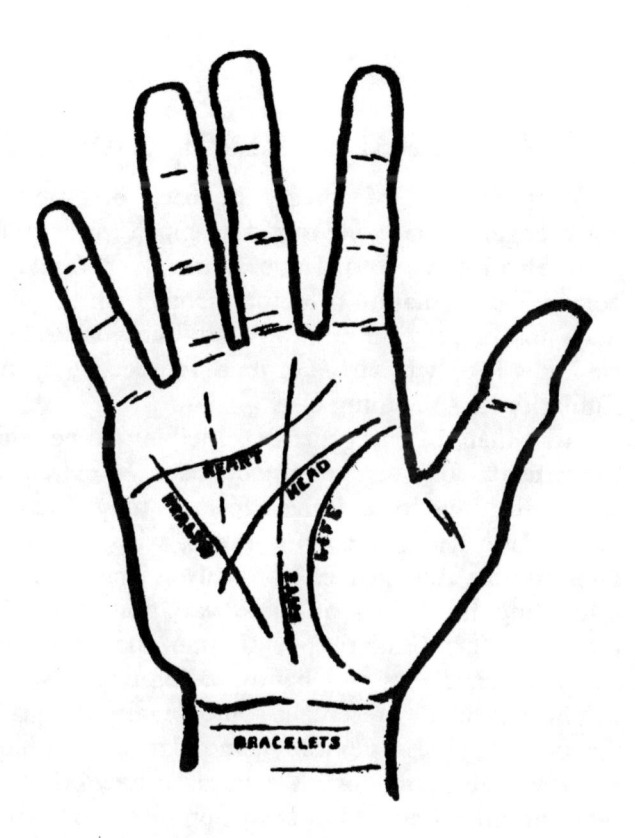

General Diagram showing the Principal Lines of the Hand

GENERAL PRINCIPLES.

Comparison is, of course, the basis of all exact knowledge. In fact one might go much further and say that all exact knowledge is merely a carefully considered tabulation of comparisons. In the ultimate analyses we do not know anything, in itself— we know it only by virtue of its difference from, and similarity to, something else.

First, then, in our general principles comes this fundamental one of comparison between extremes. The indications to be derived from a study of hands tends always to approach a mean, with, at times, considerable divergences from this mean. It is in estimating the values of these variations that the greatest difficulties arise, and upon their accurate analysis the success of a hand reading depends.

Thus all hands present, in some degree, the qualities of smoothness, flexibility, and elasticity—which we are enabled to postulate because they bring to mind at once the ideas of their opposites. The first of these qualities is associated with the texture of the skin. For the purposes of Palmistry the back of the hand is examined for this qualification. Flexibility is largely a question of bony articulation and ligament adjustments. Elasticity of the hand may be tested by its response to the grip of another hand.

Now it is evident that texture, articulation, and

reaction to pressure are natural qualities inherent in the material of the physical organism. They must, therefore, be considered to give indications of natural tendencies or capacities. They are the birthright, so to speak, of the individual, which become, however, largely modified by his method of life, both mental and physical.

An individual with a fine textured hand may be regarded as being possessed essentially of a refined nature. And this will be found to modify the significations drawn from other indications from other sources. A very smooth, fine texture of the skin would annul to a considerable extent conflicting evidences found elsewhere. On the other hand, a rough, coarse texture would emphasise indications of insensitiveness to the finer qualities of life which might be found elsewhere.

Flexibility of the hand and fingers is an indication of similar capacities in the mind. A suppleness of the joints is correlated with mental activity that enables the broader view to be taken, because of the capacity to see both sides of a question or situation. The absence of this quality betokens, generally, a mind that is more rigid and unbending—that has decided upon its course and neither desires, nor intends, to forsake it, even if fresh evidence be afforded it.

Elasticity of the hand, which is shown by its power of response to the grasp of another, and the quick reaction to the pressure put upon it, denotes a mind that is reasonably active, energetic, and adaptable to new conditions or fresh calls made upon it. This type of mind is one that rises superior to ordinary circumstances and the assaults of ill-fortune. The owner of this type of hand is usually trustworthy and able. On the other hand, one that lacks this quality of elasticity, a hand that is flabby and immobile, most usually denotes an idle temperament, without the desire for strenuous life, inconsistent and inconstant and deceptive, because of the lack of individuality and character.

Next, perhaps, in point of importance, comes the shape of the hands as a whole, and the shape of the fingers. Hands may be divided into broad and long, and general indications are derived from these. The long hand usually indicates capacity for detail, and in a measure mental strength, the broad hand the more dashing qualifications associated with physical strength.

Much more importance is given, however, to the shape of the fingers, and the character of the finger tips. These are usually designate as pointed, conic, spatulate, and square, while the fingers are described as long or short, smooth or knotted, according to their prevailing characteristics.

Pointed finger tips indicate generally those of an artistic temperament, who, however, sometimes lack the ability themselves to do great things unless other indications are found of powers of application and activity. Usually these persons are of dreamy disposition. Conic fingers are indicative of the impulsive and instinctive types, who, while likeable in their general qualities, are sensitive, prone to exaggeration, restless and volatile, prone to rapid changes in their outlook, pessimistic and optimistic by turns.

Spatulate finger tips denote those fond of outdoor life, energetic and self-confident. Usually original and resourceful, they care little for conventions, and are frequently found to be successful because enterprising and active. Square finger tips are the possession of practical and methodical persons, who are ruled mainly by reason and custom. Punctuality and order are generally associated with this type of finger tip.

If the fingers and hands generally are smooth and long, the outstanding traits are generally those of impressionability, of inspiration and intuition.

Knotted hands, that is those in which the joints particularly swell, indicate powers of analysis, order, reflection, and a leaning towards philosophy and scientific speculation.

Each of the fingers is held to correspond to one of the planetary significations in astrology. Thus, the first finger, the forefinger, is that of Jupiter, the second that of Saturn, the third that of Apollo, and the fourth, or little finger, that of Mercury. The fingers, therefore, according to their modifications and shapes, give temperamental indications of great value.

For the thumb great claims are made. Some experts will be prepared to give a delineation of character almost wholly based upon the shape and contours of the thumb. Its three phalanges are respectively held to be, beginning at the top, indicative of will, reason, and love. These, it is seen, correspond closely with the psychological analysis of the mind, as will, understanding, and emotions—the three making up the great trinity of faculties or powers.

From the appearance of the hand, when it is held open and without restraint, general deductions as to the powers of the mind are drawn. If the forefinger and second finger are furthest apart independence of thought is suggested. If the third and little finger are widest apart independence of actions is seen. If both intervals tend to show a wide space these powers are aggregated, as self-reliance and originality.

If the thumb inclines inwards towards the other digits this is an indication of avarice; if it inclines outwards generosity is to be deduced.

If a hand be examined it will be seen that instead of a regular surface the palm presents small plateaus here and there. Some of these are much more prominent than others. Some clearly represented on one hand are perhaps entirely absent from other hands, and *vice versa*. From the presence or absence of these "mounts," as they are called, general indications are drawn.

Usually seven mounts are dealt with, viz., those of Jupiter, Saturn, Apollo, Mercury, Mars, the Moon or Luna, and Venus. As might be inferred, the first four mounts lie at the bases of the fingers after which they are named, beginning with the forefinger. Midway down the palm, just beneath the mount of Mercury, comes that of Mars, and below that of Mars, nearer to the wrist, comes the mount of Luna. The mount of Venus lies, opposed to that of Luna, at the base of the thumb.

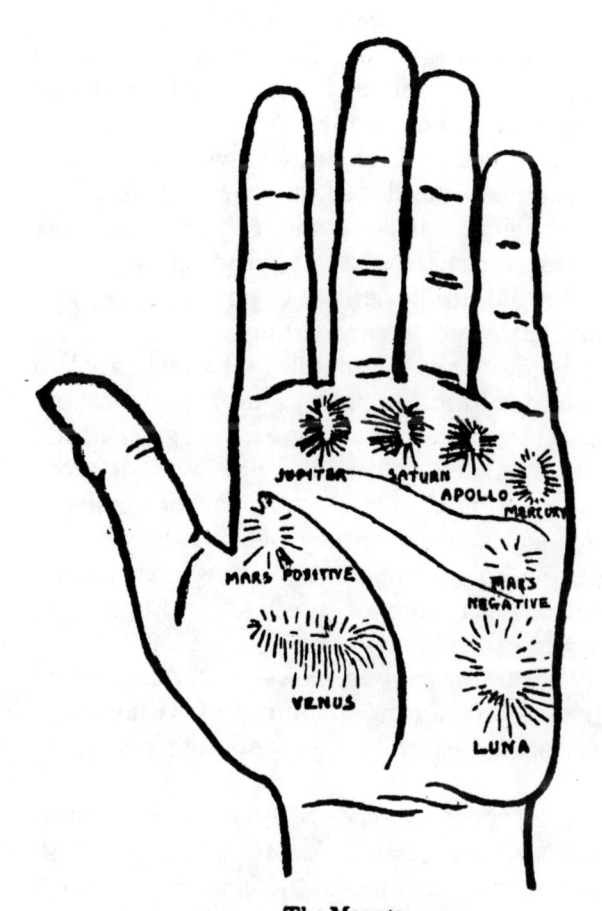

The Mounts.
Mars Positive = Aggression.
Mars Negative = Resistance.

Each of the mounts, like each of the fingers, shows the absence or presence of general qualities, and their extent or negation. An example will make this clear. If the mount of Jupiter be well developed we may expect to find in the subject the qualities of laudable ambition and religious convictions. If the mount be poorly developed, or absent, it would indicate irreligion, idleness, and vulgarity. On the other hand, an excessive development of the mount of Jupiter would indicate love of power, pride, and religious fanaticism or superstition.

Here, then, we see a principle that must be applied in all readings from the palm; a normal indication, by reasonable shape or development, suggests certain qualities associated therewith. Excessive development increases what may be good qualities in themselves to such excess that they become vices. The absence of such development gives negative indications—there is a lack of positive quality and a tendency to exhibit its antithesis.

Every virtue pushed to excess becomes a vice; the absence of normal qualities of virtue open the way for the exhibition of opposing characteristics.

Associated most closely with the ideas of most persons who have given Palmistry a thought at all is the notion that the lines of the hand are the most important. It was in order to contradict this comparatively wrong impression that we have dealt first of all with the other indications to be obtained, and to show that a good delineation of the character, which after all is the principal thing in guiding the destiny or fate, may be obtained without consulting the lines at all.

But as the lines may be held to give indications of actual events to come, it is very essential that they should be dealt with fully, if cheiromancy or prophetic hand reading is to be indulged in.

There are many lines in the hand, some naturally considered to be of more importance than others. The principal are the lines of life, of head, of heart, and of fate. The lines of fortune and fame, of health, and of intuition are also held to be valuable whilst the bracelets, as they are termed, of health wealth, and happiness are not to be neglected.

Most of the principal lines are self explanatory so far as what they indicate. A general principle to be used in delineation is that a "good" line is one which is narrow, deep, and of good colour. An undefined line, broad and shallow, and of indeterminate direction, negates all the good points that might otherwise be indicated by it. In these lines there may be breaks or stars, or masses of criss-cross lines. Each of these has its special significance and will be dealt with later.

It used to be the fashion, amongst popular exponents of Palmistry, who had, however, little justification for their theory because of the lack of their. exact knowledge, to read only from the left hand As this was nearest the heart it was thought, by these persons, that it was likely to be in more intimate association with the life principle.

Close study of the art reveals, however, that both hands should be read, first separately and then in conjunction. The left hand usually conveys the indications which the subject may be considered to have inherited. The right hand gives the modifications arising out of the habits of the life itself.

This is only as it should be, since the right hand practically obeys the dictation of the life principle by carrying into effect, moment by moment, all that is willed by it. In some cases immense divergences are to be observed between the indications of the two hands, showing how much the growing character has been able to impress itself upon what was otherwise the course of fate.

OF HANDS IN GENERAL

If we now regard the hand as a whole, we may take it that very valuable indications may be drawn from a complete survey of it, ignoring for a moment the lines and mounts. We shall be able to arrive at a fair estimate of the character and general tendencies—the raw material, so to speak, from which the destiny depends.

First, then, should be studied the relation in length between the fingers and the palm, and between the various fingers themselves. Those persons whose fingers are short in proportion to palm length, are usually impulsive, and act largely upon instinct rather than upon reasoned processes. Short fingers, with large nails, indicate those who are averse from detail, as they appear quickly to grasp a complete notion of the subject, and object to wasting time upon minutiæ. Short fingers, with small nails, indicate those who, though disliking detail, will attend to it.

Long fingers indicate a less rapid judgment, with more attention to detail, and greater ultimate accuracy, with reasoning processes that enable both sides of a question to be worked out before the conclusion is reached. Small nails are suggestive of the critical faculty, methodical work, and organising power, particularly if the joints are well developed.

A normal hand exhibits a definite and formal relation of lengths of the various fingers. But very few hands entirely conform to this standard. Some of the fingers are longer or shorter than the normal would require. This, then, is the root point, to ascertain which is the dominant finger, or fingers.

Then, too, there are normal lengths for the phalanges, which are sometimes exceeded or not reached. The dominant phalanges should also be looked for. Each of the fingers, as was said before, signifies a group of qualities, and the dominant will be one of the great determinators. So, too, with the phalanges; each of which has its own particular qualifications.

If we take the fingers in order, the first or forefinger is that of Jupiter, and if this finger is dominant in the hand—that is, if it is the longest finger in proportion to the normal length—Jupiterian qualities will be in excess in that hand, and will be exhibited by that character. Its three phalanges indicate, beginning with the first, or nail phalange, religion, ambition, and love of rule.

The second finger, that of Saturn, for its three phalanges connotes mysticism or melancholy, love of outdoor pursuits, and material longings. Saturn is the planet that rules the earth, and those in whom this finger is dominant may be expected to show a fondness for the grosser and less idealistic views of life.

Next comes the finger of Apollo or the Sun, and when this finger is the dominant one, it may be inferred that the nature of the subject is cheerful and

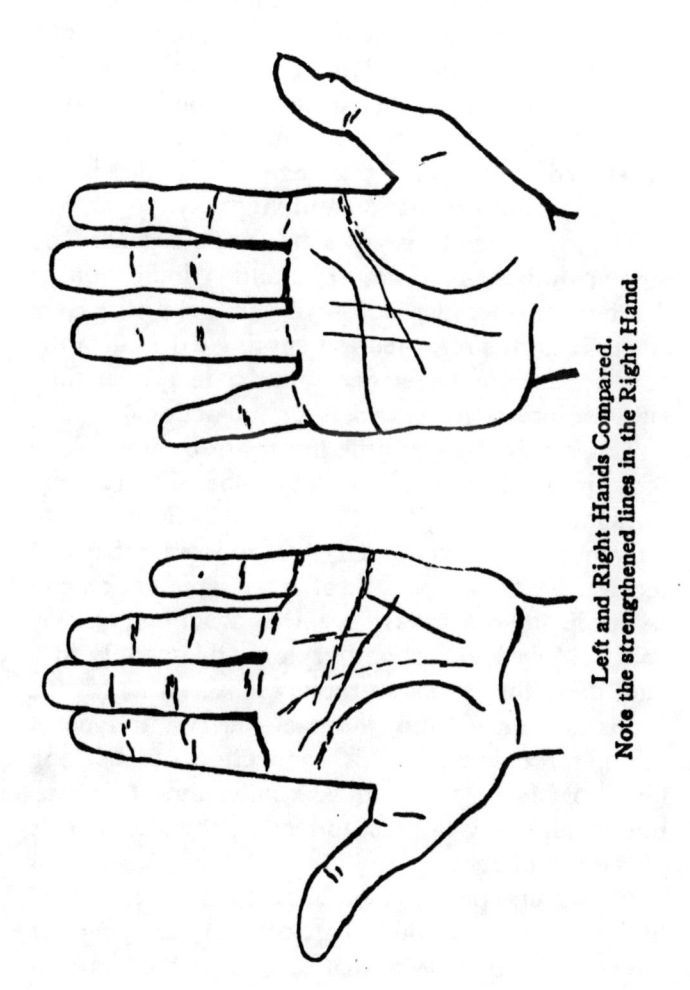

Left and Right Hands Compared.
Note the strengthened lines in the Right Hand.

bright, sunny and optimistic. The Apollo finger is that which indicates the possession of artistic talents, If the first phalange be dominant there will be trace of excess in hopefulness. The second phalange indicates reason or caution, and should be well developed. The third phalange of Apollo, if too long, indicates ostentation and vulgarity.

The little finger, that of Mercury, is regarded by some palmists as an almost infallible indication of the temper and disposition of the subject. Here again, length is regarded as denoting a person prone to remember and feel deeply for a length of time either injury or the reverse—a good action.

Those with a short little finger are thought to be those in whom the outburst of temper is very fiery, but soon over. So, too, they would be less likely to remember, or to feel acutely the kindnesses they had received. They would be of more rapid action and reaction. Quick to take fire, they would as quickly cool. Moved to respond rapidly and warmly to a kind deed, they would as rapidly lose its after effects.

On the other hand, those of the slower type of mind, represented in this connection by the long finger of Mercury, would take some time to rouse, but equally long to react to lose all the after effects of the impulse.

A long first phalange of Mercury denotes a great flow of language and a capacity for carrying the crowd. It would seem that so great is the power of the orator that he or she can convince the hearers almost against their reason.

When the second phalange of the Mercury finger

is both long and thick, this denotes a power of perseverance that will enable its possessor to triumph over many obstacles. But a long and thick third phalange shows an individual with contemptible characteristics that may, in excess, indicate cunning, deceit, and dishonesty.

Other indications drawn from the little finger are its degree of curvature. If this is great it seems to promise the sensibility and sympathy that are essential for nursing.

In addition to the indications drawn from the appearance of the hand when held free and open (these points were dealt with briefly in "General Principles"), some general deductions of value may be made from the way in which the hands are carried as the person walks.

Benham indicates no fewer than fifteen types, from the deceitful, dishonest individual, who hides, or tries to hide his hands, to the philosophic individual who carries his behind him in a pose that is absolutely unassumed. The artistic temperament is shown by a graceful carriage of one hand partly raised to the waist line, or above it.

A cautious individual usually has the hands at least partially closed as they swing at the sides. The bully clenches his, but in a manner different to that of the miser.

The lackadaisical individual is detected at once by the aimlessness and droop of his hands at his sides as they swing helplessly. The brisk, sharp temperament is seen in the carriage of the hands with some indications of forcefulness in their pose.

A student will quickly detect for himself many little things in this way as his powers of observation ripen. The indications are there waiting to be tabulated and classified.

But indications of this kind must, of course, be subject to the confirmation of the other details, abstracted from a consideration of the shapes of the hands and fingers and a close study of the lines and mounts.

It may be thought that all this complicates the art. This is true; but therein lies its value. If it were possible to say that just this or that observation would give a reading more or less accurate, one would be inclined to doubt its efficacy. There is no royal road to success in Palmistry.

If one is to get reliable results from it, and these can be obtained, it is by the careful observation of multitudinous details, checked at every point, and compared one with the other. The human character is a mass of complexities. Its destiny depends upon the working out of some of these complexities.

And if one desires, even in mathematics, to obtain a solution to a problem, there are many calculations to be made, additions, subtractions, multiplications, divisions and cancellations to be effected before the end heaves in sight.

So, too, with Palmistry. We may, of course, make a rough and ready approximation. A minute's study will suffice to give a few of the outstanding features of character and destiny—a glance at the shape of the hands and finger tips, and at the lines and mounts, will enable one to do this.

But who would care to sum up the physical and mental characteristics on a five minutes' acquaintance? In either case you could make a bold outline, and this might be reasonably true. Yet, if a detailed portrait of the individual were required, it would be necessary to have many sittings and a very close intimacy.

The reader, therefore, must be prepared to encounter many little difficulties that may crop up in his study. There will be many apparent contradictions. But when all the points are viewed as a whole, a portrait will become visible which will give the light and shade, the moulding and the outline of the form as a living entity, instead of a bare outline that seems more or less lifeless and merely approximate.

OF LINES AND THEIR CHARACTERISTICS.

So far we have dealt with general principles, and also with the character indications to be deduced from the general conformation of the hand, and the shapes and character of the fingers. Now it is necessary to deal with something that makes a more insistent appeal to the average person.

We refer here to the lines, from which indications of very great importance are to be obtained. There are many of these lines in the hand to which special attention is given in detailed works on Palmistry. In a small book of this kind it is not possible to enter into such minute analysis.

Here, then, we propose to take six of the more important lines, viz., those of the Life, Heart, and Head, and the lines of Fate, Fortune, and Health. Naturally, the names of the lines themselves determine largely the nature of the particular influence they exert upon the individual's destiny.

The Life line, for example, gives a graphic record of the general nature of the life. According as it is steady and well cut, and without signs of joints or ruptures, so it is deduced that the life will follow a reasonably easy course. The line of Heart indicates the course of the affections, and in many cases

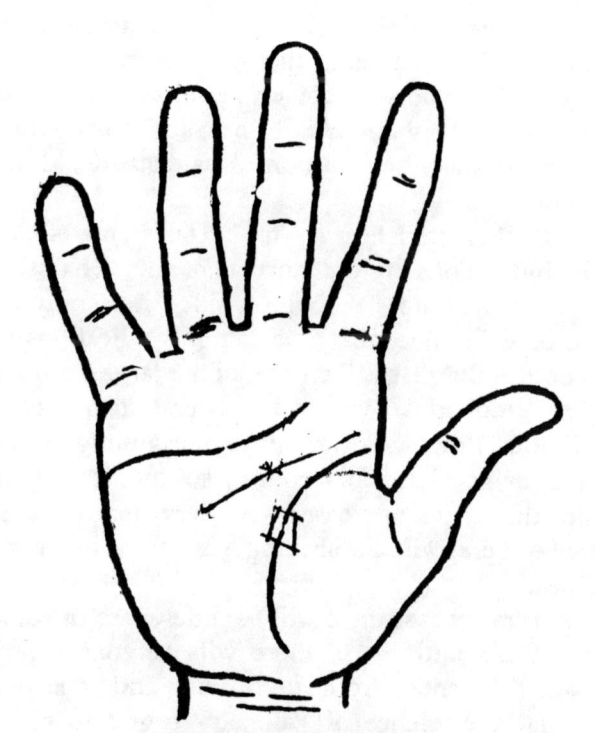

**Breaks, Squares and Stars.
Note the opened Fingers.**

is united closely in general contour with that of the Life line.

The Heart line generally indicates the emotional capacity for love in the individual in the same way that the line of Head indicates the intellectual abilities and attainments that pertain to the individual. The line of Fate or Destiny is one that intersects the Head and Heart lines, and usually runs partially parallel, for a portion of its distance, to the Life line.

These characteristics are to be taken merely as broad indications of the normal hand. That this must be so should be obvious, since it is only by virtue of differences that one can get indications of variation. But just as there are, in the large majority of cases, individuals whose life course is one easy continuous flow, with very little outstanding events to mar or accelerate its course, so too, it will be found that in many cases—in very many cases indeed—there will be striking similarity in broad outlines.

But in every case there will be differences of some sort. Here and there, there will be found very marked differences from the normal, and it is just here that the science of Palmistry begins to make itself of value. It is in determining the meanings of these variations, whether they be great or small, that it justifies itself as a science.

Reference was made before that both hands should be consulted. An old fallacy was that which spoke of the left hand as being the best from which to read. As was pointed out, the left hand must not be neglected. Indeed, it is most valuable as showing the natural or hereditary tendencies upon which the environment or fate is to play its part. The right hand frequently shows a great difference in its markings, and even in its formation, from the left hand, by virtue of its work done, modifying the tendencies with which the subject started.

This is partly the case with regard to the major lines—those of Life, Heart, and Head. The subject may have started with an hereditary tendency to a calm and untroubled existence. A change in circumstances, a change in environment, brings him or her under fresh influences. There are great emotional stresses, larger opportunities for intellectual advancement, and these mutually react upon one another, so that great modifications are apparent in the right hand.

Some general indications here may be given. The lines should be deep and clear and even. This implies that the characteristics indicated are continuous and forcible. On the other hand, if the lines upon close examination show that they are subjected to, here and there, breaks and differences in depth and colour, this may be regarded as a sign of lack of purpose and intensity.

Broad, shallow lines are indications of unfavourable characteristics. The lines which, while continuous, show in their course a branching off, indicate attempts which have been made, but unavailingly, to change the general character of that life.

One meets, in many instances, a line which is continuous but not constant in depth and colour. These, too, show that at varying periods the purpose of the individual has varied in intensity. These general remarks are applicable, it will be seen at once, to most of the lines.

For detailed reading it is necessary to have some means of ascertaining at what periods of the life these breaks or changes occurred. Reference to details on a later page will show a scheme for the general allocation of ages. This must be taken in general terms, and must be checked by the palm reader by his own experience.

Sometimes the line is seen divided and then re-united, leaving in its course what is called an island. The significance of this is fairly easily seen. It is that something has happened to obstruct the main current, but not sufficiently to stop it, but rather to force it round the obstacle in diverse directions and then re-unite by its own power of overcoming resistance.

In other cases squares are found. The main line is seen to be broken, but enclosed on both sides of the break by bounding lines which form a complete box, from which the line has no power to discharge itself. It would seem, then, that the box or square is the productive agent against the danger that is implied by the cessation of the line.

Benham adheres very closely to electrical analogy, and likens the square to an electrical contrivance, or safety box, by which the current, otherwise in danger of breaking away or discharging, is confined within this area, and finally allowed to discharge itself through a continuation of the main line.

These squares must be distinguished from islands. The latter are breaks in the main stream which afterwards re-unites. The current flows along two independent channels, but then rejoins of its own accord, as it were. The island is significant principally of divided impulses at that period.

" The island," says Benham, " is always a defect, always a disturber, a warning to look out for something, and must never be disregarded." The square, on the other hand, may be regarded as "a protection from danger, and a repair agent of certainty and reliability."

Dots are sometimes found in the lines, or close alongside them. These indicate breaks and alternations, and denote diseases which have interfered, more or less seriously, with the course of the flow of the life for example; if in the Life line, or if in the Head line, with intellectual difficulties and embarrassments. Dots, for example, in the latter line have indicated deafness and dumbness, or heart disease.

Occasionally one finds a line that may well be likened to a chain. It is, for part of its course at least, a succession of links of varying depth and intensity. This, in the Head line, would indicate a lack of intellectual purpose, disturbed undoubtedly by physiological causes, tendencies to headaches, and other brain stresses, likely to result in a poor or vacillating purposiveness.

Cross bars, short lines that cross at right angles, or thereabouts, the main lines are to be considered a danger, a menace to the even flow of the current in that line. Their seriousness will be denoted by their comparative depth and colour. If deep and overlined they are a source of trouble. But if merely outlined and lightly etched in, they must be noted, but are not really serious.

A mark that is fairly frequently found in hands is the star. It is always important, and must not be overlooked. Its significance depends largely upon its character. It may record either an illumination, a quickening, as it were, of the faculties concerned, or an explosive capacity that threatens the most grievous danger.

If the star is a small, well-defined mark, evenly lined in and nicely proportioned, without actually causing a break in the line, it indicates the intensifying of that line in a brilliant exposition of its qualities at that time. It is the emphasis and culminating point of the career.

But if the star be large, badly formed, diffused, and the line is broken violently near its centre, with a dot for the star centre, this is a mark that denotes a very dangerous period. On the Life line it will indicate possibly a sudden death. On the Head line it will denote an excessive brain storm that may well terminate in insanity.

A cross is a fairly common sign. It is a single bar across one of the principal lines. Like the "cross bars" it is to be read according to its depth and intensity of colouring. The cross is a defect which may be comparatively unimportant, or may become a real danger to the purpose and meaning of that line.

Sister lines are sometimes seen. These are lines running parallel, or nearly so, to a principal line. Their importance depends upon their own strength compared with the weakness of the line they support. If the main line becomes weakened or broken, or poor in definition and colour, the sister line affords it valuable support. Even a good line becomes better by the presence alongside it of a sister line.

PRINCIPAL LINES.

1. LIFE, HEAD AND HEART
2. FATE, FORTUNE AND HEALTH

As was said in reference to hands in general, Palmistry is a comparative study. It depends upon the departure from a normal or average conformation of the hands or lining of the palms for its interpretation of the great differences to be found in human character and disposition and destiny. As there are very many hands that are relatively true to type on both counts, so there are very many individuals whose disposition and fortune follow an almost absolutely even destiny from cradle to grave.

But, on the other hand, there are also a great many persons who vary very considerably on every point from the normal. There are others who present striking and outstanding features. There are others again whose careers and capacities are so striking that they can scarcely be grouped at all. They form a class by themselves, and even then each individual differs from all the others. They are only a class because of their essential and radical differences on varying points from all the others.

In order, therefore, to give a basis for the divergences from the normal, we must lay down the course

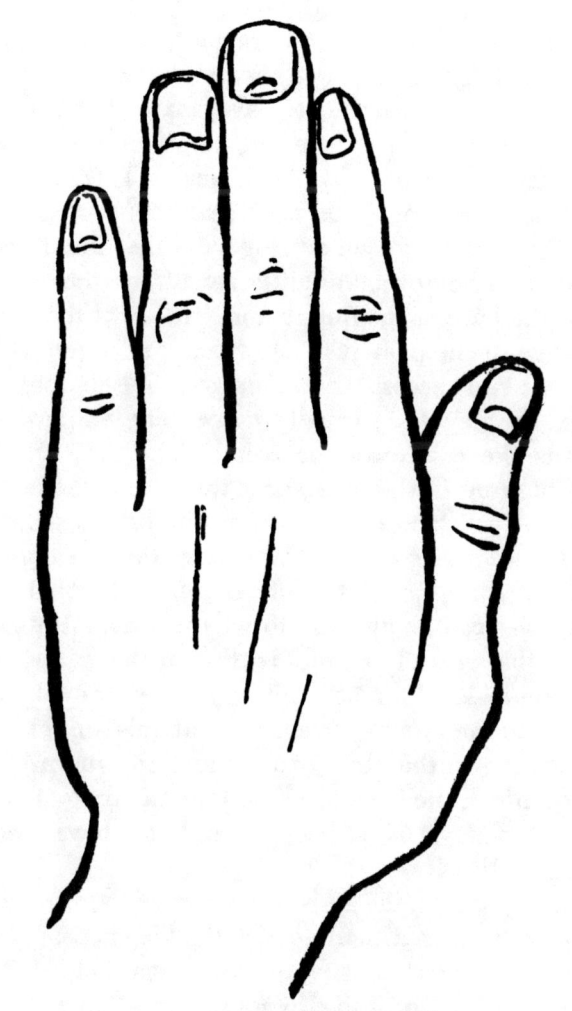

Fingers Square and Pointed.

of the principal lines and then suggest how the various divergences from them may be interpreted.

Our first figure (No. I) indicates these principal lines. For convenience, to save space that would be taken by another illustration, all six of the principal lines are given, viz., the Lines of Life, Head, Heart, and Fortune, Fate, and Health.

In this section we are dealing with the first three of these. The normal life line runs from the wrist round the base of the thumb and finishes at the outside edge of the palm just below the head line. The head line runs across the palm from its beginning above the life line, usually descending somewhat towards the centre of the palm. The heart line starts high up in the palm, near the base of the forefinger, or just beneath it, and runs across the palm.

It is sometimes asked, "Why does the line of life show the duration of the life of the individual?' No answer can be given as to why it does. But an answer that is really helpful is this—if the palms of all individuals who reach old age be examined, in every case the line of life shows that this might be expected. On the other hand, those in whom the line of life is neither significant nor definite have almost as invariably been found to have had shortened lives.

In other words, the basis of predictive Palmistry is the hypothesis that the lines are the life map of the subject. Each exhaustive reading has helped to establish the truth of this hypothesis and to render it more and more an exact science.

There are very few cases in which the life line

is entirely absent, though in some it is seen to be very poorly marked—in cases almost indiscernible. In these instances it is safe to anticipate that the subject is one who is never in a robust condition, whose life hangs delicately suspended, and may be terminated easily at any period.

Although this may be taken as an indication of a poor life, it may sometimes be found that a very strong head line, in conjunction with great will power—shown in the thumb—will outweigh the weakness of the life and ensure its continuity. Some persons live on almost by will, in spite of a very weakly constitution. The life line must be taken as an indication specifically of its own sphere.

When the life line rises high up on the hand, from the mount of Jupiter, this shows the life to be an ambitious one, with very strong desires. The tendency of these particular desires will be shown by the dominant fingers and mounts.

The course of the life line should be noted. If, for example, it runs in close to the thumb, and thereby restricts the mount of Venus, the subject is probably cold, unsympathetic, and lacking in desire for intercourse with the other sex.

When the life line tends in the other direction, well into the palm, it indicates warmth, passion, generosity, and other emotional characteristics that are conducive to long life and energy in intercourse.

A long life line must not be regarded as an infallible indication of a long life. It denotes in general the vigour and natural health of the subject. But if, for example, there are on the other lines of head or heart signs of disaster, these, in themselves, may indicate a breaking up, or even the earlier death of the subject. In many cases, of course, the life line itself shows the break, or star, that may denote disruption or death. In other cases, as cited, these signs may be found elsewhere.

A marked difference may be seen at times between the life line in the two hands. When the stronger line is found in the right hand this indicates that the course of life is in favour of lengthening its natural, or inherent, period. The reverse is the case if the right be weaker than the left. The life is being shortened by its mode of living.

If the life line be thin and narrow the subject will have less vitality and vigour. This does not necessarily mean weakness or ill-health so much as less capacity for resistance to hardship and exposure.

A broad and shallow life line indicates a subject who is usually deficient in muscular power and physical vigour. This should be remarked especially if the other lines seem to be good and strong. For then the constitution will be unfitted to support the efforts of the life, and despondency and misery may well result in the disposition. These are the subjects who take their own lives.

It is not unusual to find the early part of the life line "chained," or broad and shallow, and then later, developing into a deep, fine, strong line. This is sometimes to be remarked in a comparison of the two hands. This shows a weak childhood, with a strengthening in vigour and robustness as youth and maturity are reached. An example of this is shown in the illustrations.

A break occurring in a good life is not necessarily an indication of a shortened life. If the line is really good its own momentum will carry it over the break if the other lines confirm this.

There is little reason to doubt that the Line of Head actually indicates the mentality of the subject. So many experiments have been made, and all of them seem to support this view. It is a line which is very rarely absent, though cases have been known in which it could not be seen. If the head line be short and the life line is short also, it may be reasonably assumed that the life period will be shortened. A bad star ending either or both these lines may be regarded as a certain indication of fatality.

If in the left hand there is a shorter head line than in the right, it may be inferred that the life is threatened at least mentally.

In reading the head line, care should be taken to isolate the defects due to disease from those due to character. If the head line is defective—if it has breaks, islands and dots—the source of these must be looked for elsewhere. They will indicate, if found also in the health line, for example, that physiological stresses are affecting the mentality.

Often the head line begins alongside, sometimes coincidentally with the life line. Soon it is seen to start independently on its own course. Where this occurs quite early in its run, it is a sign of an early start in mental capacity as an independent unit.

Conversely, where the lines run together for some distance, it may be inferred that there is less display of independence in youth. Some show complete severance, indicating self-reliance from infancy.

Separated head and life lines indicate sensitive people, and where the head line is seen to rise near the mount of Jupiter, it denotes a capacity for leadership, with a natural tact that makes for success. A straight unvarying head line indicates one whose purpose is fairly fixed, and the more evenly balanced is the individual, with practical and common-sense views.

When the head line perceptibly curves upwards towards the mount of Saturn, this denotes one in whom the tendencies are towards material success in finance, mining, or farming. If the head line be deflected towards the mount of Apollo, then the subject will exhibit artistic capacity, or even love of display.

A wavy and uneven head line shows a lack of fixity of purpose, changeability, and absence of self-reliance and originality. The opinions of such persons are not consistent. They vary without due cause. If the head line runs close up to the heart line it will show one whose course is more dominated by the qualities of heart than of head.

When the head line is seen to merge into the heart line it shows an individual in whom the emotional tendencies constantly predominate. The judgment and mental qualities are largely at the mercy of the impulses which arise in the emotions.

A head line that runs up to the mount of Mercury

shows one who is inordinately fond of money-making—who will devote his talents to this, and perhaps prove a very hard employer. On the other hand, where the head line runs down towards the mount of Luna, there will be imagination—a valuable quality for speakers, writers, and linguists.

Sometimes the head line forks, portions running off towards the mounts of Mercury, Mars, and Luna.

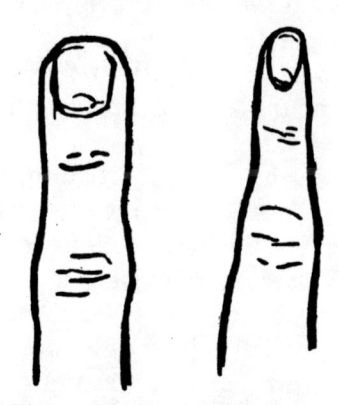

Fingers Spatulate and Conic.

Such a marking is very favourable, as it indicates versatility and great mental activity.

Much of what has been said above of the two chief lines refers also to the Line of Heart, which, by the way, some palmists consider almost the most important.

Of the Line of Heart, Benham says:—"There are three well-verified readings attached to three starting points, and these should be used as the basis for your work, modifying and changing them in accordance as you see the starting points vary.

Rising from the mount of Jupiter we read the development of the sentimental side to the affections. The subject is one whose love is ideal, to whom love is an adoration, and to whom love, even with poverty attached, is ideal."

When the line "rises between Jupiter and Saturn, the line shows the common-sense, practical, middle ground with the affections, indicating one who is not carried away with sentiment, but who views love from a practical standpoint, is not soft or spoony, but who is inclined to think that love in a cottage, without plenty of bread and butter, is a myth."

"Rising from the mount of Saturn, the marking shows the sensualism in the affections of one whose love is tinged with the idea of pleasures from sexual relations." This is particularly true if the other indications, a large mount of Venus of pink or red colour, and with strong life and heart lines, confirm it. The three main indications given above show how to distinguish the affections when ruled by sentiment, practicability, and passion.

If the heart line drops considerably towards the head line, this shows one in whom the mental faculties will endeavour to rule the affections. This will be strongly emphasised if the head line be more firmly marked than the heart line.

A reading is assisted if a broad indication is first obtained of the type to which the subject belongs. If the Jupiterian or Saturnian or Mercurian qualities seem to prevail generally, head may well rule heart.

But if the subject be either Apollonian or Venusian, if these qualities be in excess, then the heart will probably prove stronger than the head.

A short heart line indicates a failure in the affections, and may even indicate a stoppage of the heart itself—an end to the life, if other indications bear this out. In any case it denotes a growing selfishness and coldness. A heart line that runs right across the palm shows one who will be ruled by sentiment, even to the risk of his business.

Now it is important to note here that the age at which the particular defect or strengthening, the deflection or renewal of a line's course occurs, may be told within reasonable limits by measuring the line into a series of years or epochs. Taking as a basis the length of a normal life, for example, as seventy years, a rough division of this at the centre would give thirty-five years each way. The point should be fixed in the mind's eye. For one half of the length of the line which is seen in any particular palm obviously cannot be taken, since the life line might extend to ninety or more, or might be shortened to one half that age.

This is the means which is used. A normal type of hand—an average hand—is used as a diagram, and upon this is laid down a scale. The other lines are treated in the same way, sub-divisions being put in at pleasure to divide the line up into periods of three or five or seven years. Important changes in health or fortune may thus be measured and foretold pretty accurately.

2. LINES OF FATE, FORTUNE, AND HEALTH.

A reference to the diagram will show the position of these three lines. It will be seen that they run almost vertically, instead of horizontally, as the lines of heart and head do, roughly speaking.

Taking first the Line of Destiny, or Fate, this will give an idea of the general course of the life from a material point of view—it will show the good or evil fortune of the individual. It generally has its termination—it is measured from the wrist to the finger—in the direction of the mount of Saturn, and is sometimes called the line of Saturn.

Those who take advantage of opportunities are frequently those who are spoken of as lucky or fortunate. Frequently it happens that by foresight they have appreciated or intelligently anticipated what was likely to happen and seized the golden moment.

Usually, therefore, those with a good line of fortune, or fate, rather, are also endowed with a strong, and good head line, indicating the possession of valuable mental qualities that enable them to create even the opportunities for a successful career and a fine destiny.

In some cases the destiny, or fate line, appears to be almost entirely absent, and yet these have been very successful persons. Benham suggests that these are self-made persons, whose initial equipment in the way of destiny was little; they were in quite humble circumstances. But by dint of their own energy they have carved out a place for themselves.

When the fate line rises inside the line of life

success seems to be assured, partly by the assistance of friends. But when it takes its rise in the centre of the palm success is assured by the sole efforts of the subject. A rise from the mount of Luna seems to indicate assistance from the opposite sex. This has been noted where careers have been helped by wives, for example.

A line that starts well up in the palm indicates little material advantage in the earlier years of life. If the line is good thereafter it seems to promise things almost wholly as the result of the subject's own efforts.

Breaks in the line indicate failure of efforts, and if found principally in the right hand, these are due possibly to acquired habits. If deep and thin alternately this indicates periods of depression and prosperity, and care should be taken that all that is gained in the one should not be lost in the other.

The Line of Fortune, or of Apollo, because it runs towards that mount, seems to indicate the possession of some of the qualities that Apollo confers, such as brilliancy—Apollo is the sun—which may be shown either as success in the arts, or fame and success in some other direction. Benham suggests that a good name for this line would be that of *capability*.

The possessor of it—it is not always found, being very frequently quite missing — is one who has the possibilities ever before him of shining in one or other of several directions. Just how he will shine depends largely upon the other characteristics displayed by the hand.

If no line be present this does not indicate an absence of success in life. But if present, and as a good line, it does intensify very largely the prospects of success. It is the line which makes effort easy. The lines of destiny or fate, and of fortune, may be regarded in a measure as sister lines. They afford support to one another.

Finally, we come to the Health line, or line of Mercury (see diagram). This indicates generally—as does the life line—the constitutional weakness or strength of the subject. A bad line of health, shallow, uneven, wavy, broken or deflected, promises, as will be obvious, many indispositions and sicknesses.

Various disorders are attributed to the many indications observable in the health line, but with these we cannot well go into detail. It must suffice to show generally what may be deduced from its appearance, as has been done above.

THE MOUNTS

1. JUPITER, SATURN, APOLLO, AND MERCURY.

In judging mounts both hands must be referred to. The left hand will frequently give an indication that is considerably altered in the right. In some cases this results in a development which is promised in the left hand failing to take place. In other cases it is the reverse. The left hand shows only a very small development of a mount or mounts, which in the right becomes very pronounced.

It will be found on examination that many hands show strongly marked mounts, some quite normal mounts, and others, depressions where the mounts should be. A good upstanding mount naturally means that its particular qualities are to be found plainly evident in that person. The normal type of mount would indicate one in whom those qualities would be basic, but less clearly expressed, and not so dominant in the character. The absence of a particular mount would denote that the qualities which are deficient will lead to other modifications of the subject.

Usually it will be found that one or other of the mounts is the most prominent, though sometimes cases occur in which two or more mounts seem to strive for mastery and only achieve equilibrium.

The first thing to do, then, is to discover which of the mounts is the dominant.

Four of the mounts lie at the bases of the fingers after which they are named: those of Jupiter, Saturn, Apollo, and Mercury. Of the others, that of Venus lies at the base of the thumb, and Mars and the Moon respectively lie on the opposite side of the palm, Mars beneath Mercury, and the Moon mount beneath that again, but there is also another Martian mount to be found alongside the mount of Venus within the life line.

These seven mounts indicate generally the classes, or types, to which humanity corresponds.

Jupiterians, those in whom the mount of Jupiter is plainly the dominant, are ambitious masterful, and usually capable of leadership. Benham thinks there are really very few *pure* Jupiterians. The true Jupiterian is a very strong and forceful type, but is nearly always found alloyed with something else. Jupiterian qualities in excess are, of course, bad.

Saturnians are the type of person whose action is that of a balance-wheel to the other types. Saturnian qualities are a useful sort of brake upon the others, preventing them from going too far or too fast. The Saturnian qualities are essentially repressive if in moderation, but if very pronounced they become bad.

Normally the Saturnian is a sceptic, a cynic, and a student. He tries all things before he trusts anything. He withdraws himself from society, is fond of the earth rather than of his fellows, studies physics

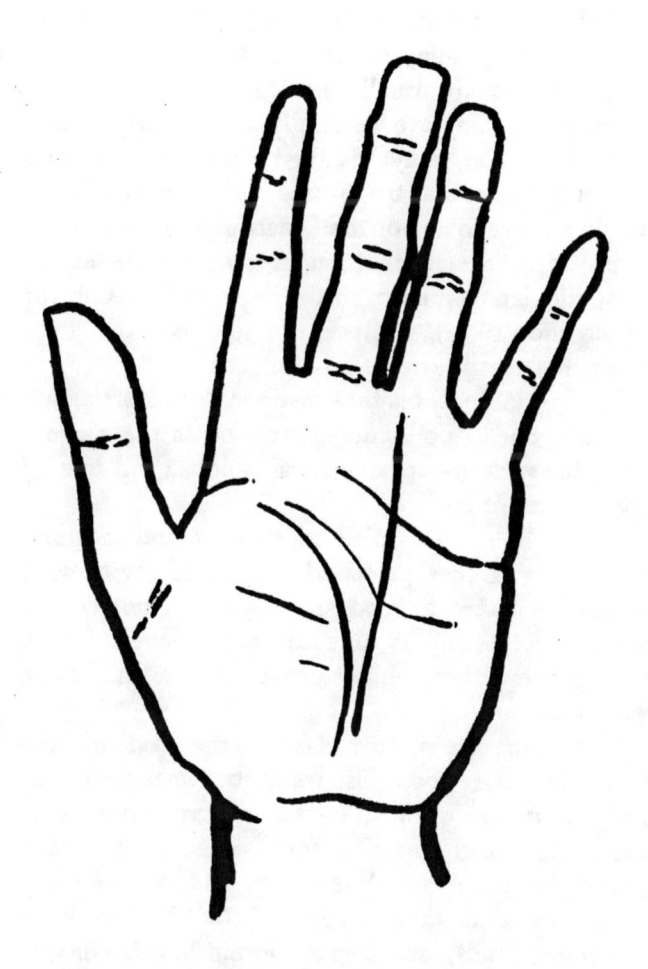

A Mixed Hand, with Smooth and Knotted Joints.

and the laws of nature. He is inclined to be miserly, and is usually gloomy in his outlook in life.

Apollonians are usually healthy and vigorous; in consequence, they are generally genial, bright, and attractive. They may be called the sunny type, who see the lightness and brightness of the world. They are always the lovers of the beautiful and the artistic. It has sometimes been thought that the possession of Apollonian character means necessarily genius for the creation of art. This is not so. But the great artists are nearly always Apollonians.

The special features that distinguish the artist are a really good Apollo finger, as well as the mount; the latter with its apex central, and a good line of Apollo in addition.

An Apollonian is quick in thought and imagination, but is neither profound nor deep. With what he has he makes a good show. He is not economical, but usually is able to make money freely. He is sometimes unfortunate in his marriage relations.

Mercurians are of two classes—the good and the bad. On the good side may be instanced such qualities as shrewdness, facility of expression, tireless energy, and capacity for judgment of human nature. If these are diverted to bad ends we can easily see that they may lead to all manner of deception, fraud, and lies. Herein lies the danger of the Mercurian type. "He is adroit, crafty, and a constant schemer," says Benham, "using all his powers of shrewdness, intuition, and oratory to get himself through the world. He is a clever manager, and knows how to keep in the background or push forward some puppet to do his bidding."

Most successful as a physician, the Mercurian usually gets a lucrative practice. In this his qualities of judgment and shrewdness and intuition are valuable as an aid to diagnosis. Mercurians are largely found, too, amongst *successful* business men.

2. Mars, Moon, and Venus.

As was said before, there are two mounts of Mars, the upper and the lower, or the positive and the negative. These two mounts may again be regarded as indicating the particular qualities associated with aggression and resistance.

Martians are therefore fighters in the largest sense of the word. They may not fight always with lethal weapons—generally speaking, most soldiers and sailors are Martians—but they will be found to possess those qualities that broadly we classify as those of a fighter.

Those who lack these qualities are the unsuccessful ones in life. For without power of resistance and even of aggression, there can be no success and good fortune. This does not mean that those who do possess a good supply of Martian qualities will be successful. It merely shows that they will fight and resist. Generally the Martian is well-disposed, spends his money freely, and is a good and staunch friend.

Lunarians, those in whom the mount of the Moon is dominant, are naturally nervous, restless, and lovers of change and travel. They are imaginative, idealists, and easily form mental pictures. In this type are found linguists, musicians, and writers of romance. A lack of this mount indicates a dull mind that denotes the clodhopper.

Physically the Lunarian is lazy. He is the dreamer rather than the man of action. He is a mystic frequently, and often borders on the melancholy. He is sensitive in response to external influences, and quickly moved by ideas or dreams or visions. "If of a common type," says Benham, " he has a hard time to get along." But with other good qualities to back them the Lunarian makes use of his imaginative faculties and bends them to his purpose. A lover of nature, the Lunarian is often a sailor—the sea is his particular medium. In music he likes the profound and classical rather than the light and gay melody. He is cold by nature and inclined to be selfish and self-contained.

Last come the type of Venus. In this, too, we must distinguish between two diverse classes—those in whom the good qualities of love are marked, and those in whom its baleful, reversed qualities are apparent.

Generally speaking, the Venusian type are remarkable for sympathy, generosity, warmth, and attractiveness. In this type there is little of gloom or selfishness. Strong physical characteristics are present which make for life and love and beauty. There is constant attraction present for the other sex, and strong qualities of head—in the head line—are desirable if a good balance is to be preserved. The Venusian is of cheery nature and joyous habits.

A smooth mount indicates a love of flowers, music, form, and colour. If the mount be grilled, that is crossed with fine lattice lines, it indicates strong sexual passions that need holding in check.

Benham says you will never find a full mount of Venus without a love of melodious music. If the mount and finger of Apollo indicate also artistic capacity, the Venusian quality will show its development in music.

It will be seen from the above that each mount possesses its own qualities—taken collectively they are complement and supplement. Each is modified in some way by others to some extent.

CONCLUSIONS

A short summary and a few hints may be helpful. In giving a reading, do not allow some prominent characteristic to lead you to express a hurried opinion upon it. Remember that each hand must be read as a whole and both together. The writer has found the following a fairly safe method to pursue.

Glean, first of all, what indications you can from the carriage of the hand and the nature of the personality, and then taking the hands both together, examine them for a minute or two to form a first general impression.

In doing this note quickly the shapes of the thumbs and fingers, the texture of the hands, the class of joints, shape of finger tips, and dominant fingers and mounts.

You may explain to your subject to cover this period, that you are examining the hand for general characteristics, to obtain a balanced idea of the more prominent indications.

Then taking the left hand, go over this briefly to see what was promised by innate tendencies, which may then broadly be described. Thumb, fingers tips, and joints, and then pass on to lines and mounts.

It will be found, as you go, that the general statements tend to become more and more modified, but more and more specific.

When you turn to the right hand, to follow out the course of the life which has been pursued, you will already have laid down a fairly good plan upon which to impress your details.

Now you are able to become more and more definite, since all the previous indications begin to aggregate and to show the prevalence of some particular characteristics which emerge as the features of the character.

If you wish to give a very detailed reading, it will be necessary, of course, to study some of the other books mentioned herein, Benham's, Mrs. Robinson's, and Cheiro's.

Benham is full of detail, largely on the physiological side, whilst Mrs. Robinson gives some good ideas of predictive Palmistry. Benham gives good diagrams for placing the age of various events, and should certainly be consulted by those who desire to become quite proficient in this most entertaining art

Printed in the United States
134392LV00002BA/23/A